OTHER BOOKS BY DOUGLAS JOHN HALL

Hope against Hope (1972)

The Reality of the Gospel and the Unreality of the Churches (1975)

Lighten Our Darkness: Towards an Indigenous Theology of the Cross (1976)

Ecclesia Crucis: Church of the Cross (1980)

Has the Church a Future? (1980)

The Canada Crisis: A Christian Perspective (1980)

The Steward: a Biblical Symbol Come of Age (1982)

The Stewardship of Life in the Kingdom of Death (1985/88)

Imaging God: Dominion as Stewardship (1986)

God and Human Suffering (1986)

When You Pray: Thinking Your Way into God's World (1987)

The Future of the Church: Where are We Headed? (1989)

Thinking the Faith: Christian Theology in a North American Context (1991)

Professing the Faith: Christian Theology in a North American Context (1993)

Confessing the Faith: Christian Theology in a North American Context (1996)

God and the Nations [with Rosemary Radford Ruether] (1995)

The End of Christendom and the Future of Christianity (1995)

Remembered Voices: Reclaiming the Legacy of "Neo-Orthodoxy" (1998)

Why Christian?—For Those on the Edge of Faith (1998)

Etre image de Dieu: Le stewardship de l'humain dans la creation (1998)

The Cross in Our Context: Jesus and the Suffering World (2003)

Bound and Free: A Theologian's Journey (2005)

The Messenger: Friendship, Faith, and Finding One's Way (2011)

Waiting for Gospel: An Appeal to the Dispirited Remnants of Protestant "Establishment" (2012)

What Christianity Is *Not*

What Christianity Is *Not*

An Exercise in 'Negative' Theology

DOUGLAS JOHN HALL

CASCADE *Books* · Eugene, Oregon

WHAT CHRISTIANITY IS *NOT*
An Exercise in 'Negative' Theology

Cascade Books
An Imprint of Wipf and Stock Publishers
199 W. 8th Ave., Suite 3
Eugene, OR 97401

www.wipfandstock.com

ISBN 13: 978-1-61097-671-8

Cataloging-in-Publication data:

Douglas John Hall, 1928–

What Christianity is not : an exercise in 'negative' theology / Douglas John Hall.

xviii + 176 p.; 23 cm—Includes bibliographical references and indexes.

ISBN 13: 978-1-61097-671-8

1. Theology. 2. Negative theology. 3. Christianity—Essence, genius, nature. I. Title.

BT60 .H31 2013

Manufactured in the USA

FOR

Anne-Sophie Catherine Hall

Daniel Alois Johann Friedrich Hall-Kircher

Samuel Keith Hall

Rebekka Rose Daniels

Jakob Ernest Christopher Daniels

Kyle Tucker [Chaim] Daniels

Olivier Solomon Thayendanegea Hall-Gauthier

Sophia Rachelle Hall-Gauthier

"All faith systems have been at pains to show
that the ultimate cannot be expressed
in any theoretical system, however august,
because it lies beyond words and concepts.
But many people today are no longer
comfortable with this
apophatic reticence."[1]

~

Bonhoeffer was convinced that Western
Christianity is "so soaked in
religious consciousness" that
the question of "what Christianity really is"
will find answers only after
years of intense theological struggle.[2]

1. Karen Armstrong, *The Case for God* (New York: Knopf, 2001), 320.

2. Partly paraphrased from Larry Rasmussen (with Renate Bethge), *Dietrich Bon-hoeffer—His Significance for North Americans* (Minneapolis: Fortress, 1992), 67 (italics added).

Contents

Dedication

TO MY GRANDCHILDREN

Beloved Children,

I am dedicating this book, which I intend to be my last, to you. To my own astonishment, I have become an old man; and like most grandparents I spend a good deal of my time these days wondering about the future—*your* future—which I shall not see. Whether the world of tomorrow will be better than yesterday's world, or worse, no one can say; but that it will be different from the eighty-four years I have known so far is obvious enough. Some of the problems we have already experienced—problems of the environment, of the difficult encounters between nations and peoples heretofore isolated from one another, of the enormous and indecent gap between rich and poor, of the use and abuse of our limited planetary resources: some of these and similar problems will probably increase in your lifetimes, or become yet more complex. One can only trust that there will be enough human ingenuity and wisdom in your generation and those to follow that the human species will find the will and the courage to embrace and act upon the best dreams of the past.

Part of that past, the Christian faith, has occupied most of my adult years on this good earth. You all know that I have been a theologian, that I have written numerous books about Christianity, have taught many students and given many speeches, and so forth. But you have not, I suspect, understood very much about what Christianity has meant to me—and to your Oma and many of our closest friends. That is, in part, because you have been too young, or too far away, for much serious discussion of such matters; but it is due also, I fear, to a fault in me. Sometimes I am bothered by the thought that my life has been spent teaching other people's children, whilst my own dear children and their families received only bits and pieces of the enormous treasury of the faith and hope that I struggled to comprehend—often, indeed, you received these bits and pieces from a tired and preoccupied man, who was glad enough to find diversion from his labors in the small and great pleasures of family life.

I regret this, because I know that at least some of the wisdom that you will need for the living of your lives in that complex world that the future will be can come from the contemplation and practice of the faith-tradition that has shaped so much of our Western world. Personally speaking, I don't know how I could have faced the ordinary challenges of life, to say nothing of the great historic crises of the almost-century during which I have lived, without faith in a God who is both *with us and for us!*

But unfortunately—and this is what concerns me most—this same faith tradition that has guided me and countless others is itself imperilled in our time, and many of the forms in which it comes to you and your cohort are terribly misleading. Often, indeed, some of them are just silly—spiritually cheap and intellectually debased. I am not referring to the fact that for a century and more Christianity has suffered losses of numbers and influence and power: if you one day read some of my other books, you will find that these quantitative losses do not greatly trouble me. They are in any case inevitable as the Christian religion ceases to be the official or established religion of most Western nations. What is far more troubling are the *qualitative* losses: the trivialization of Christianity, its reduction to very simplistic ideas and slogans, its failure to speak to the most complex problems and anxieties of human beings—to the point that many of the most sober and thoughtful men and women of our time no longer find in this faith anything profound enough to wrestle with, or even to pay attention to. This represents an agonizing dilemma for thinking Christians today, because so very much of the Christianity they hear and see and are bombarded with today makes them ashamed and embarrassed; for it is simply not the faith to which they have devoted their minds and hearts

Modern media, which have aided and abetted this bombardment, will not overcome this dilemma; to the contrary, its increasing dominance of our culture only aggravates the problem. Last night I watched a television report that celebrated the glories of the multifarious and ever-expanding communications systems and devices for the spreading of religion in the world today. With the flick of a finger, prayers can be called up for every sort of occasion; whole bodies of sacred writings can be flashed before one's eyes in an instant; religious services of every shape and kind—from the pomp and circumstance of Rome or Canterbury to the gospel sway-ings of spiritualists and the rants of evangelists—circulate without ceasing throughout cyberspace and can be tapped into at any moment. Individu-als can be connected—can have church!—without ever setting foot in a building or being present with other flesh-and-blood humans. Christianity, Judaism, Islam, Hinduism, Buddhism: they are all, and much besides, im-mediately and effortlessly . . . available!

Dear children, do not be fooled by this smorgasbord of religion. It is not all bad, or wrong, but it falsifies, in its total affect, what the human quest for spiritual depth is all about. Not only Christianity, but every profound religious tradition, requires of people—if they are at all serious about it—a great deal of reflection, study, thoughtfulness, listening, speech, and silence (sometimes called prayer). Many hours will have to be spent in solitude, many words will have to be read and pondered, many conversations will have to be engaged in; there will be times of great uncertainty, doubts will assail one, anxious questions will never be wholly absent. And even after eighty-four years one will have to confess that one understands very little (almost nothing!), and in all probability that one's faith is also very, very small.

But one will know, at some profound level of consciousness, that one has been a human being—*ein Mensch*. Aristotle defined humans as "ratio-nal animals." And Augustine of Hippo added that such *thinking* animals would inevitably be "restless" until they could find something greater than themselves to think about. All great religions (and this the only reason they may be called great) manifest both of these characteristics of genuine hu-manity: that is *thought-filled,* and that its thought, if honest and persistent, leads it beyond itself to that which it can honestly devote itself—or, in other words, can love.

Christianity has suffered the humiliations of all great religions in the contemporary world; perhaps it has suffered more than any of the others. There are complicated reasons why that may be the case. As the dominant religion of the most powerful nations and empires of the world, from Rome to America, Christianity has been associated in the minds of many non-Western peoples with the imperial civilizations of the West. Many Chris-tians or former Christians themselves have become critical of the Christian religion because of its record of power seeking, its attempts to Christianize other peoples, and its too-easy dismissals of alternatives to itself. You will see, if and when you read this or other books of mine, that I have a certain sympathy for such critical assessments of historical Christianity.

But the greatest humiliations of Christianity have not originated with worldly doubters and critics. They have arisen within the Christian church-es themselves. Too many avowed Christians, often the most enthusiastic among them, have mistaken some *aspect* of the Christian faith for its very center. Thus, you will be told by some very fervent believers that to be a Christian you must "believe in the Bible"; some will even say that you must accept every word of Scripture as absolute truth! Others whom you will likely encounter will insist that you can only claim Christianity as your faith if you belong to the church—and usually they will mean some particular church or denomination.

There will of course be many too who will tell you that Christianity involves strict adherence to a code of morality. Usually they will be quite specific: Here are the rules! And you will be puzzled, quite understandably, because others who eagerly announce their identity as Christians will pres-ent you with a very different set of rules.

Another group, having perhaps recently encountered some of the many other religions, whose numbers and influence will certainly increase in your time, will tell you to hold fast to Christianity because it only is the Truth. Perhaps they will argue that our country—or our civilization, or the Western world—is the most advanced in the world because it is Christian. They will certainly dismiss the atheists and agnostics, who have gained a certain hearing in my time and will probably become even more visible in yours.

I could go on. All such advocates of Christianity—even the sincere and very nice ones, for there are many such—have mistaken some *aspect* or *component* of the Christian tradition for its essence, its core or center. They have elevated the Bible or some code of ethics or the church or certain doc-trinal truths to the highest position in the life of faith. They do this, usually, because these *components* of the faith are relatively concrete and graspable. We can get hold of them—and use them for our own purposes, purposes that, alas, are often quite self-righteous and even bellicose. Besides, many people, perhaps most, find it too baffling and too daunting to embrace a faith whose center is a living Being, and therefore a profound mystery whom we can never possess or fully understand but only . . . *stand under.*

I have written this book with you and your generation in mind be-cause I want to help to preserve *that* center. If I have learned anything in my long life, it is that everything—*everything*: God, the Creation, the myriad creatures and processes of life, indeed life as such, and we humans who have been given the wherewithal to contemplate it all—everything is steeped in ineffable mystery. And if I were asked to say, in a word, what Christianity has contributed to this awareness of mystery, which has been felt by all great philosophies and religions and sciences, I would answer that Christianity professes and confesses that at the center of this universal mystery there is . . . *love*. Eternal, forgiving, expectant, suffering love.

That is why the life, death, and resurrection of Jesus, called the Christ, is the central image and narrative of the Christian faith: because his story announces so poignantly and unforgettably how love, despite all that negates and demeans it, is the origin and end of all that is: the *alpha* and *omega*, as the Scriptures say.

If we, the thinking animals, once experience something of this love (and most of us experience at least intimations of it—in our own loves), we shall know perfectly well that we can never rightly explain it. But we shall also know what it is not. And that knowledge will make us question everything that is put forward, or that puts itself forward, as though it were ultimate, the last word. Christians are skeptical about all alleged last words, because the only last word they honor is a Word that was "made flesh and dwelt among us," and a Spirit that lives among us still—*appearances notwithstanding!*

Beloved children, may you, through all the adventures, crises, joys, ups and downs of your lives, be and become more and more conscious of *that* Word, *that* Spirit. To be sure, it is a Word that defies translation into words and a Spirit that, like the wind, cannot be seen. But if and insofar as it touches your life, you will find rest for your souls and a peace that passes understanding.

Lovingly,
'Opa'
Notre-Dame-de-Grâce, Montréal
A.D. 2012

Preface

WITH THE BREAK-UP OF Christendom, serious Christians throughout the globe find themselves confronted in new and urgent ways by the question, *What, really, is Christianity?* Shorn of its 'religious' accretions, what remains of this faith-tradition? How, as Christians, can we remain faithful to the core of the gospel whilst opening ourselves in modesty and compassion to others who are "not of this fold"?

In its quest for religious certitude and political ascendency, Western Christianity in particular has too often ignored or obscured the transcendent mystery that gave and gives rise to faith in the first place. 'Negative' or *apophatic* theology aims to preserve that mystery through the development, in the Christian community, of a critical vigilance that recognizes the tendency of the penultimate to claim ultimacy. Thus this theology critiques many things held sacred by believers—such as conventional cultural assumptions, moral codes, doctrinal systems, ecclesiastical polities, and even the Bible—in order to keep faith focused on the One who cannot be reduced to codes or systems, ideas or words.

In this book I have tried to apply this theological method to the question historical providence has put to all of us who claim Christian identity in this post-Christendom world: *What is Christianity, really?* While the book necessarily reflects its author's North American identity, it aims to speak to and for the global—or, better, the *ecumenical Christian*—situation. The various 'provinces' of what was once 'Christendom' experience somewhat different aspects of the overarching question, and at differing levels of intensity, but the great problem is addressed to all of us. With the disintegration of 'the Christian religion' can we say, finally, meaningfully, what Christianity *is?* Or at least what it is *not?*

D.J.H.

Introduction

Si comprehendis, non est Deus.

ST. AUGUSTINE

RELIGION IN A VIOLENT WORLD

ON THE 12TH OF September, 2001, the following paragraph appeared in the English newspaper the *Guardian*:

> Many of us saw religion as harmless nonsense. Beliefs might lack supporting evidence but, we thought, if people needed a crutch for consolation, where's the harm? September 11th changed all that. Revealed faith is not harmless nonsense, it can be lethally dangerous nonsense. Dangerous because it gives people unshakable confidence in their own righteousness. Dangerous because it gives them the false courage to kill themselves, which automatically removes normal barriers to killing others. Dangerous because it teaches enmity to others labelled only by a difference of inherited tradition. And dangerous because we have all bought into a weird respect, which uniquely protects religion from normal criticism. Let's now stop being so damned respectful.[1]

A much shorter version of the same message appeared on the wall of the Presbyterian College in Montreal in the form of a huge graffito. It read simply, "RELIGION KILLS!" All of us who taught in the Faculty of Religious Studies at McGill had to walk past this taunt. That particular wall had borne many other antireligious slogans over the years, but this one was punctuated by the dramatic collapse of the Twin Towers in Manhattan, an image seared on all our minds. The graffito didn't single out any one

---

1. Richard Dawkins, copied from an article on Dawkins in *Wikipedia*.

religion, though we all knew that it had been a debased form of Islam that had inspired the event of 9/11. In our Faculty, most of the great religions of the world were represented, some more prominently than others; so the accusation was intended for—and, I think, felt by—all of us.

Nor has that message been lost on the general populous. Professor Richard Dawkins's statement in the *Guardian* makes sense to a great many people, and though Dawkins is famous for his "new atheism," more than a few of those of us who eschew atheism find much to commend that statement; for, as Christians, we have our own quarrel with religion, as I shall explain presently. The current resurgence of public interest in atheism, agnosticism, and secular humanism has been stimulated by the dastardly events of 9/11, but it has been lingering beneath the surface of public consciousness throughout the Modern period. The horrifying image of the collapse of the World Trade Center towers has only pinpointed and made concrete a disdain for religious zeal that has long been a subtheme beneath the song of technological triumph that our civilization has been so lustily singing. Now the subtheme, roused not only by 9/11 but by a whole host of catastrophic occurrences (perhaps the most *characteristic* occurrences of the twentieth century and beyond!), has risen to a pitch and, for many, quite drowned out that old triumph song. Until now it has been possible for most people, even skeptics and agnostics, to assume that on the whole religion is a good thing. But when so much of the planet's violence seems inextricably bound up with religion, this assumption is increasingly questioned by large numbers of people. It does not take great insight to come to the conclusion that if indeed "religion kills" or creates attitudes that may well result in the degradation and destruction of life, it would be better to avoid religion, or at least to exercise a certain caution in that area. This too contributes incalculably to the exodus from the churches, especially from those churches that have encouraged people to think for themselves.

In the face of this renewed questioning of religion, many who are committed to a faith tradition are prone to become defensive. Typically, their defense, when it is not just emotional, draws upon three observations: (1) While, throughout recorded history, religion may have caused occasional harm, its major contribution to human civilization has been positive. (2) Religious factions that create or foster hostility and violence are usually distortions of the faiths they imagine they are serving. (3) Very often where religion is blamed for destructive attitudes or events, the truth is that the religion is being used to bolster causes that are ideologically or politically driven. For example, few if any informed persons believed that "the troubles" in Northern Ireland were really the consequence of genuinely Catholic and Protestant agendas, even though the media invariably referred to the situation in those terms.

Such defense of religion is legitimate enough when it is sensitively stated; but it rarely gets at the heart of the problem. For the problem is not only that religion is frequently misinterpreted and misused; the problem is that there are dangerous and vulnerable spots in most if not all religious faiths, which, if they are not recognized and their practical effects closely monitored within the communities holding these faiths, are likely under certain social conditions to become vehicles for the expression of suspicion, prejudice, fear, or hatred of others. And the really subtle aspect of all this is that such dangerous and vulnerable spots in a religious system cannot be confined to those rather obvious places where religious belief treads a fine line between strong personal faith and bigotry with respect to others; rather, such flash points can and do emerge in connection with the most apparently innocent or seemingly positive affirmations of a faith tradition. It is obvious enough, for instance, that a religious community that blatantly excludes from salvation or fullness of humanity any who do not consent to its self-same dogmas is actively courting conflict with others. But it is not at all obvious that belief in a deity whose compassion abounds, or a sacred text that marvelously illumines the mind, or a moral code that affirms the unique value of each individual, or a faith community in which human mutuality and unity are fostered—it is not at all obvious that such highly affirmative and apparently humane affirmations of faith might be or become the spiritual heritage out of which a religion . . . "kills."

Immediately within the ecumenical Christian community itself, however, we have witnessed over the past four or five decades how it happens that precisely such well-established and seemingly salutary teachings of our faith can become the occasions for tension, alienation, and the exclusion or oppression of minorities. The central figure of Christianity—the Christ—pictured by pietistic and liberal theologies of the nineteenth century in the most gentle and inclusive terms, has been perceived by significant numbers of Christians and others a century later as an excluding representation of the divine: as a white, male image of God, the Jesus of ecclesiastical doctrine and practice has conveyed to many women and non-Caucasians an extension and legitimization of patriarchy and Western domination. Moreover, his cross, the chief symbol of the faith, has been felt by significant numbers of thoughtful Christians to valorize suffering and impede the liberation of marginalized people. Again, the prominence of *anthropological* interest in the Bible, which heretofore was taken for granted and even lauded, began— in the face of the crisis of the biosphere and the degradation of the natural order by aggressive Western technocracy—to seem to many a highly questionable and even perilous anthropocentrism.

In short, we have been through a period of intense scrutiny of our faith, a quest for its unexamined assumptions, its implicit biases and hidden messages. Most of us over the past thirty years have learned—a little—to listen to the words of Scripture, liturgy, hymnody, theology, and preaching with the ears of others: women; racial, ethnic and sexual minorities; economically or otherwise disenfranchised people. We have not achieved all we should have in this respect, but some significant practical and attitudinal changes have been made, at least in liberal and moderate Christian circles.

But it is, one suspects, only a beginning. Not only is the habit of self-critical reflection on our beliefs and pronouncements limited to a minority of thinking Christians, albeit a significant minority, it is still very much an in-house phenomenon. I mean that those of us in the churches of Europe and its satellites who *do* ask how our faith and witness may be heard by others have still not encompassed in our horizon of consciousness *those* others who exist outside the boundaries of our more conventional, more familiar occidental sphere. To some extent, we have learned since World War II to listen to our own preaching and theology with the ears of Jews: the catastrophe of the Holocaust, together with the testimony of the Jewish community in our midst, have awakened us from our centuries-long sleep with respect to Christendom's active and passive roles in the sufferings of its parental faith. In a less consistent manner we have begun to recognize, some of us, the role that our religion has played in the humiliation of the indigenous peoples of our continent and the planet at large. Certainly more of us today have learned to listen to Christian doctrinal and moral teachings—for instance on marriage and sexuality—with the ears of persons spontaneously inclined toward members of their own sex. In these and other ways, speaking at least for significant minorities within the remnants of classical Protestantism, I think it may be said without undue exaggeration that our awareness of those who are other has expanded significantly by comparison with the past. We *are* more inclusive in our thinking today—not only in terms of whom we welcome into our congregations but in terms of our basic perception of the great variety of human life: of the multitude out there who hear or overhear or partially hear or *mishear* what we are saying and praying and singing and writing in our churches and Christian councils, and who are affected, willy-nilly, by what we say and do, and do not say or do.

Still, I think we should have to conclude that this consciousness of others is only in its initial stages, for the multitude out there is much greater and more diverse than we have yet been able to grasp. I suppose we shall never grasp it fully, for the contemporary, wired world is indeed a *multitude*; its diversity is scarcely imaginable, yet in its immense variety it is no longer far away but part of our immediate environment—as any five-minute surfing of the Internet demonstrates. The mandate that is issued to Christians, in this opening up of the great world that we call globalism, means that we shall have to *attempt* a more informed consciousness of and compassion for the *entire* world than Christianity heretofore has ever had, or even felt that it ought to have. For without such consciousness we shall never be able even to formulate our witness, let alone to anticipate the effects of our witness, for good or ill, on those who hear it—all of whom, regardless of race or clime or creed are, according to our faith, beloved children of God.

In other language, *ecumenical thinking* in the future Christian movement will have to be almost infinitely more expansive than it has been before. The *Oikoumene*—the known world—for the early church meant the territories, tribes, and peoples clustered around the Mediterranean Sea. After the sixteenth-century European discoveries of new lands, even whole continents, the *Oikoumene* had to be enlarged, and this enlargement has continued apace throughout the centuries ever since, as knowledge of the planet and its vast spaces and myriad cultures grew. Moreover, we know that this expansion of the *Oikoumene* has not been an easy or automatic process, so far as the church's intellectual and emotional appropriation of it is concerned. It is one thing to discover a new fact about the world, for example to find out about cultures heretofore unknown; it is something else to absorb such facts to the point of letting them affect our thinking—including our theologies. Such absorption requires time. Religious communities taking shape initially within well-established and *relatively* monocultural frameworks (such as the Roman empire or, later on, the European community of nations and their colonies, or nineteenth-century America) quite naturally reflect the mentality of their geopolitical context; and it takes a very long time for religious communities to transcend their cultural conditioning long enough to take in, mentally and spiritually, the new, enlarged world of their present. Euro-American theology and ecclesiastical policy still today has conspicuous difficulty encompassing in its purview even the reality and the meaning of theologies developed in Latin America. For most of us in the West, the whole southern hemisphere and the Orient, including the near East, remain virtually *terra incognita*.

AVOIDING FALSE SCANDALS

This opening up of the globe that is a consequence of the combined expansion of science and technology, facilitated by modern communications, presents the Christian movement, then, with an unprecedented spiritual and intellectual challenge: the challenge to expand our working awareness of our worldly context to include lands and peoples and creatures and processes unknown by our own grandparents. We are obliged now not by something external but by our world commitment as ambassadors of the incarnate One to listen to our own theologies and sermons and liturgies and hymns and ethical counsels with the ears not only of Jews but also of Muslims (to name only one, the most prominent, of the *religious* others of our expanded global context). We are obliged by our own commitment to the *whole* of God's good creation to reflect on the implications of what we are saying or not saying in our churches and councils about the extrahuman creatures and natural processes that, on the whole, we have heretofore ignored. While our congregations in most once Christian Western lands are depleted, our listening audience, so to speak, has expanded phenomenally in this age of ubiquitous and instantaneous communications. How can we achieve an informed and compassionate sensitivity to the multitude that is overhearing us? More important, how can we open ourselves to all these others *while at the same time remaining faithful to our own foundational credo as Christians*? How can we avoid giving *false* offense, where these others are concerned, while remaining faithful to the gospel of the cross, with its own offense, its own "stumbling block," its own *skandalon* (1 Corinthians 1–2).

For that, I think, is how the question—the basic, confronting question of the Christian mission in our global context today—has to be formulated. This is no time to avoid the true stumbling block and scandal of our faith, which is certainly inextricably bound up with the crucified Christ. To escape *that*, to avoid *that*, would be to opt out of this faith-tradition altogether. The ultraliberalism and modernism of the late nineteenth and early twentieth centuries demonstrate very clearly that the adjective *Christian* and the noun *Christianity* are hollow and puerile if "Jesus Christ and him crucified" is replaced by some allegedly less particularized center. More important, precisely this *christocentric* center, for all its particularity, when it is deeply understood, is infinitely more inclusive than are most of the allegedly universal religious messages put forward to replace that center—messages whose *seeming* universality usually cloak highly chauvinistic and biased assumptions. The point, therefore, is not how to avoid the *skandalon* of "the crucified God" (Luther/Moltmann), but how to avoid the *false scandals* that have indeed plagued the course of Christendom throughout its history and are still extraordinarily and virulently at work today. The point is not how to make ourselves and our message, as Christians, entirely and painlessly accessible to the multitude; rather, it is to try as steadfastly as we can to ensure that what the multitude hears is really the gospel and not some culturally biased religious doctrine or secular ideology that obscures the gospel and offends and alienates others wrongly or needlessly. The point is not how to achieve superlative political correctness of the kind that forfeits, in the end, the possibility of saying anything at all decisively, lest it offend; rather, the point is to avoid elevating to the status of the essential accidental, peripheral, or secondary concerns that too easily become the occasion for confrontation, conflict, and violence.

That is why, in these chapters, my purpose will be to identify certain misrepresentations of Christianity, which, though they all concern matters indeed closely bound up with this faith both historically and doctrinally, when they are raised to the status of Christianity's essence or core confession must be perceived as false scandals poised to become flash points of conflict and alienation *vis à vis* others who are not of this fold—and also (let us acknowledge right away!) some who are of this fold. In a word, I want to identify some of these vulnerable spots of Christianity so that what this faith really is, what it *really* claims, what it wants of us, what it wants to give us—so that this *core confession* or *kerygma* might have a better chance of shining through the thick fog and darkness of the myriad claims to Christianity in today's global village.

What really is Christianity? As one who has tried over nearly half a century to answer that question in the affirmative, I can testify to the near impossibility of doing so in a really satisfying way! *But perhaps it is possible to say what Christianity is* not. It is always more difficult to say what something is, especially when that something is an organic, moving, changing historical entity, than to say what it is not. Of course we must assume some more or less integrated, if tentative or intuitive, understanding of what a thing is in order to specify what it isn't.[2] But if we can eliminate what the thing is not, we may leave, at the center, a space where *das Ding in sich* (the thing in itself) may identify itself or (to say the same thing in other language) may come to us in all its ineffable mystery. If we exercise enough nuanced care and enough modesty about our own witness to God's Word—if we "rightly divide the word of truth" (2 Timothy 2:15, KJV)—we may succeed in leaving room for the divine Spirit to fill in the holy silence that *we* cannot precisely or accurately name. That is my object here.

THEOLOGY *VIA NEGATIVA*

What is Christianity not? What, among all the many things that Christianity is reputed to be, or has tried to be, or still presents itself here and there as being, ought we to rule out? What should we eliminate from our understanding of the core or essence of this faith tradition? The methodology upon which I shall be drawing as I undertake this project is certainly not new, though in Western Christendom it has been employed with any kind of consistency only sporadically. It is called negative theology or theology undertaken *via negativa*, by way of negation. Under the nomenclature *apophatic* theology, this approach has informed much of the theological thinking of the Eastern Orthodox tradition. While a few historic theologians of the Christian West, mystics chiefly, made considerable use of the *via negativa* (one thinks of Meister Eckhart, Nicholas of Cusa, John of the Cross, and others), the West has usually preferred the *via affirmativa*, or *kataphatic* theology; that is, it has wanted to advance positive theological statements and systems—partly, one has to say, because such an approach serves more directly than any negative theology could have done the powerful hierarchic institutions of Western Christendom. Ecclesiastical establishments like papal Rome at its height, or even the less powerful Protestant state churches of Europe, seem to require equally definitive and triumphantly positive theologies. But for some sensitive Christian thinkers of the East, these Western theologies have seemed to diminish or violate the essential mystery of God and the things of God. Theologians like the so-called Pseudo-Dionysius, the Cappadocian fathers, John Chrysostom, and John of Damascus were so conscious of the ineffability of the deity that

2. See in this connection the conclusion and afterword of this study.

they found human attempts to describe God affirmatively to be lacking in humility and quite possibly to be courting idolatry. One has the impression that neither Catholic nor Protestant theology has been particularly worried about that possibility! And with hindsight, it seems to me, we might well lament the fact. Looking back over some of the immense and exhaustive systems of theology developed in Western Christendom, not to speak of such modern expressions of religious omniscience as Christian fundamentalism, one is often a little embarrassed today. It strikes many of us, I think, that too much Western theology knows a lot more about God than it should—or could! It lacks the kind of humility that contemplation of the Infinite ought surely to induce in finite creatures; and at a time when (as I've already suggested) modesty on the part of religion is no longer a bourgeois nicety but a condition for human survival, this theological omniscience of Western Christendom gives one pause. For the avoidance of giving false offense, whatever else it means, must first mean honestly recognizing the abysmal limitations of our own knowledge of God and the things of God, and therefore not putting ourselves forward as infallible authorities with exclusive claims to truth. *There are no experts where the knowledge of God is concerned!* The apophatic theology of the Eastern Christian tradition at its best is grounded, I think, in that recognition.

To be sure, all inspired and authentic theology is premised on the experience of divine revelation. The revelation that the presence of God conveys to faith, however, is not so much extraordinary and compelling knowledge (*scientia*)—and certainly it is not just information!—as it is sheer awe and humility before the holy, and the wisdom (*sapientia*) that can only be the fruit of such wonder. It is surely a sophomoric kind of mysticism that grounds itself in the sheer unknownness of the ultimate. Authentic Christian mysticism is born of the wonder that is revealed in the Christ: that the world—that *we!*—should be *so loved!* (John 3:16).

Of course exceptions arise to the generalization about Western preference for kataphatic and Eastern preference for apophatic theological approaches. I already alluded to the Western mystics, who were always a rather countercultural element in the West. Indeed that quintessentially Western theologian, Augustine of Hippo, who was perhaps the main architect of Western theology, in one of his several phases or *personae* manifests a highly mystical strain. No statement may be more exemplary of the apophatic tradition than Augustine's terse phrase, *Si comprehendis, non est Deus*

(If you [think that you] understand, it isn't God you're thinking about.)[3] It was of course Augustine's more kataphatic side, especially in his later or so-called Catholic phase that set the tone for the Western Middle Ages. During the High Middle Ages, when Scholasticism achieved what may be thought the pinnacle of kataphatic or affirmative theology, Christian mysticism was almost an underground movement; but the alternative the mystics stood for was never wholly submerged, and in fact it was found sometimes in the *personal* devotion of the Scholastic theologians themselves. Even the highest schoolman of them all, St. Thomas Aquinas, was drawn to mysticism after he had experienced a spiritual crisis, a dark night of the soul and the light that was given him in that darkness. In the aftermath of this mystical experience of the divine, Thomas told his secretary, Reginald, that he could not go on with his great Scholastic project, the *Summae*, because, he said, "everything I have written seems to me *straw!*" More significantly still, when around the middle of the fifteenth century the medieval Scholastic project ground to an effective halt, it was the mystical approach to the comprehension of the things of faith that emerged to fill the vacuum, and perhaps save Western Christendom from early dissolution.

This is not uninteresting to Protestants, because we remember that Martin Luther was profoundly influenced by some of these late mystical thinkers, especially the so-called German Mystics and Meister Eckhardt. So it is not surprising when one finds in Luther's writings a frequent and lively use of the *via negativa*. And while the mystical dimension of the Reformation was rather pushed aside by later forms of both Lutheran and Calvinist Orthodoxy, it was never wholly vanquished. In fact, I would maintain that Luther's theology of the cross (*theologia crucis*) is at its core a type of *apophatic* theology; for in its rejection of religious triumphalism (the

---

3. *Sermo 52, 16: PL 38, 360.* I was delighted to see this phrase quoted in the Christmas 2005 encyclical letter of Pope Benedict XVI titled *Deus caritas est* [*God Is Love*] (Boston: Pauline Books & Media, 2006), 53.

For a fuller examination of the thought of Augustine on this subject, see the complete translation of Sermon 52 by the Rev. R. G. MacMullen on the Internet at http://www.ccel.org/ccel/schaff/npnf106.vii.iv.html/. The pertinent passage reads: "What then, brethren, shall we say of God? For if thou hast been able to comprehend what thou wouldest say, it is not God; if thou has been able to comprehend it, thou has comprehended something else instead of God. If thou has been able to comprehend Him as thou thinkest, by so thinking thou hast deceived thyself. This then is not God, if thou has comprehended it; but if it be God, thou hast not comprehended it. How therefore wouldest thou speak of that which thou canst not comprehend?"

theologia gloriae)[4], its refusal of eschatological finality, its embrace of a faith that must not be mistaken for sight and a hope that must not be mistaken for consummation, the *theologia crucis* opts for a spiritual and intellectual humility that may claim confidence [*con + fide*] but never certitude. I was not surprised, therefore, when in conducting my research for this study I found an article that declared that Søren Kierkegaard, that extraordinary nineteenth-century spiritual son of Luther, must be considered *the* apophatic theologian of the West.

Now, as the mention of Kierkegaard, father of existentialism, suggests that what lies at the heart of the apophatic tradition is the insistent sense that where *living* realities are concerned, fullness of human comprehension and definition is *ipso facto* impossible. That is why, as Augustine's luminous phrase shows, this tradition has application first of all to the deity, for God defies containment or codification. Indeed, much of the negative theology of the mystics draws quite specifically on the biblical text, in Acts, where St. Paul addresses the Athenians on Mars Hill using as his point of contact with them the concept of "the unknown God" (Acts 17:16–17). God for biblical faith is above all a living God—a God whose *presence*—not the idea of God's existence but the experience of God's presence—is the crucial factor. God for the whole tradition of Jerusalem transcends all else, is unique, beyond compare; as Anselm of Canterbury put it in a famous phrase, *Deus non est genere* (God is not one of a species). Therefore God remains the unknown one, even when God reveals Godself—no, especially then! For, as Luther insisted, it is the revealing God (*Deus revelatus*) who, precisely in revealing conceals, precisely in manifesting hides, precisely in self-giving remains unpossessible (*Deus absconditus*). The living, self-revealing God of biblical faith transcends all our preconceptions of deity, shatters our idols and images of divinity, even the highest and most philosophically sophisticated of them, and is simply present as Thou, defying objectification, defying every attempt of ours to define and describe and specify and so (in Buber's famous language) turn this Thou into an It. It should not be forgotten that the most sacred name for God in Hebrew faith is not a proper name at all but almost a conundrum—the tetragrammaton YHWH (Yahweh), which seems to mean "I am who I am," or "I will be who I will be." Strictly speaking, this means that theology, a *doctrine* of God, is impossible!

---

4. What Luther means by *theologia gloriae* is in fact nothing more nor less than a heightened expression of affirmative theology—theology that answers everything, explains everything, leaves nothing to mystery and the unfolding of the future.

To speak autobiographically for a moment, I remember when that insight first struck me with full force. I had just begun my seminary teaching career, and the insight nearly stopped me in my tracks! If God is truly God, if God is "not one of a species," but absolutely unique, unnameable, absolutely transcendent; if we, who cannot even describe our own spouses and children without falling into graven-image making, set out to describe God, then have we not committed the ultimate blasphemy? (It was about that time, in fact, that Ursula Niebuhr said to me quite earnestly, "Theology *always* walks close to blasphemy.") I began to think, then, that I had chosen the wrong profession! But fortunately a second insight came to me. I wrote it down on a four-by-six index card, and stashed it away in the midst of a whole boxful of such cards in my study. I suppose it is still there to this day. I never look for it, but I know it is there. In fact, I remember it better than any of the other hundreds of index cards I've filed away over the years. It reads, "God permits theology." As a discipline, a science, theology is impossible, for its object is no object but a living Subject. Yet God—with great condescension and forbearance—permits it . . . for the time being. So long as we know that it is not possible, only permitted, we may try our hand at it. It's when we start thinking we are really quite good at it that we had better watch out!

What I mean to say in this homely autobiographical way is this: there must always be a prominent element of modesty, or even tentativeness and hesitancy, in what we profess concerning the knowledge of God. The Creed (any Christian creed!) should be whispered, not shouted. What prevents this modesty from becoming sheer agnosticism and devolving into theistic relativism is that, knowing and trusting God as those who sometimes feel themselves to be caught up in God's presence, we may at least identify false gods, idols, demons, and unworthy images of the divine. We may not claim for our positive statements about God anything more than awkward and hesitant attempts to point to One whom we do not understand and can only stand under; but we may (not arrogantly, not self-righteously, yet with a certain confidence) sometimes say, No, this is not God, and neither is this . . . nor this . . . nor this . . . And if we do this consistently, and especially with regard to *our own ideas and wishful thinking and fond, familiar images of God*, it may be that the Spirit who is God will now and then come to us and whisper to us reassuringly . . . (Or was it only the wind?)

So theology *via negativa* is made necessary first of all because it feels impelled—is indeed "under necessity" (1 Corinthians 9:16)—to speak of

God. And God—the God who at last allowed Moses to see his back—permits us to look for words that, transformed by the divine Spirit, can perhaps—perhaps!—bear witness to the great and holy silence evoked by God's presence to us. It is to protect and honor the Word that names that silence that we who would be theologians are under necessity to take the greatest care about *our* words—"For the ear trieth words as the mouth tasteth meat" (Job 34:3, KJV).

But while theology by way of negation applies in this special sense to the deity, the apophatic tradition extends itself also to all other aspects of theological inquiry, for it understands the whole of reality to be characterized by an aura of wonder that cannot be reduced to words, formula, description or, doctrine. Alfred North Whitehead, the father of process thought, spoke of the "livingness of things," and this fits rather precisely, I think, the mindset of this tradition. If what strikes one most about the experienced world is the life force within it—its livingness, its organic and always-moving nature—then one is likely to be less than absolute in one's descriptions and depictions of it; one will find oneself drawn to the way of negation because one realizes how little trust one can put in one's feeble attempts to do justice to "the livingness of things."

One of the (relatively few!) developments that gives one hope today is the manner in which the public perception of the world—of nature, certainly, but also of human life—seems to be moving away from the wholly materialistic, objectifying mentality of the technological society to a more organic, more fluid, more animate conception of reality. Not that the technocratic, managerial mentality has disappeared—far from it! But more of us today than was the case even two or three decades ago, I think, have embraced a worldview that looks with a certain awe upon the natural order, including ourselves within that order. Partly because we have experienced great and abiding *threats* to nature and all life, we have learned to look upon the world with different eyes. Trees are not just lumber, and polar bears are not just cute big fuzzy creatures for zoos, and the Precambrian shield is not just a barren place for mining, and the oceans are not just for fishing, and people are not just statistics! James Lovelock, instigator of the so-called Gaia Theory, believes that the planet itself is a kind of living organism, and not just a rather amazing ball of substances and processes that we may get to understand and use as we please![5]

5. See in this connection *Reintegrating God's Creation: A Paper for Discussion*. Church and Society Document 3 (Geneva: World Council of Churches, 1987). This booklet (62

This new public awareness, so far as it is able to conquer or at least counter the materialistic, technological approach to reality, is where I think religious faith must turn for human dialogue today. For faith—certainly Christian faith—shares with this mentality, even when it is driven by non-theistic or secular impulses, a sense of the great mystery of all reality as the good creation of an omniscient God. And wherever that sense of mystery is entertained among men and women, there is an opening for dialogue with faith.

---

pages) is the documentary remains of one of the most interesting ecumenical meetings in which I have ever participated. It was part of that seven-year process undertaken by the World Council at its sixth assembly (in Vancouver in 1983) and known by the phrase, "Justice, Peace and the Integrity of Creation."

In May of 1987 I was one of a small group of ten or twelve persons—scientists, theologians, journalists—who were called together by the WCC to meet for several days in a small Franciscan convent in Amsterdam. One of the other senior participants was a scientist of whom, at the time, I had never heard. His name was James Lovelock, and he had just made public what at the suggestion of his friend William Golding, the English novelist, he had named the Gaia Theory. In its briefest form, the Gaia Theory states that the planet Earth is a *living* reality, and not merely a collective of inanimate substances and processes; and that therefore our human attitude toward and relationship with the planet needs to avoid the kind of objectification or "thingification" that has in fact characterized the whole modern scientific approach to nature.

Perhaps because we were the two eldest participants in the group, James Lovelock and I quickly recognized a certain commonality in our approaches to the world—though his was of course scientific and mine theological—and we found ourselves being turned to by the others for some procedural guidance; for it was a rather amorphous group, without previous acquaintance, and we had had no briefing by the organizers.

From the start, I found Lovelock's thinking both compatible and stimulating, as, e.g., Rosemary Radford Ruether has done since: see *Gaia & God: An Ecofeminist Theology of Earth Healing* (San Francisco: HarperSanFrancisco, 1992). To look upon the planet as though it were alive, even if one had to use that term somewhat metaphorically, seemed an important breakthrough in the human attempt to find a better way of understanding both the world and ourselves in it. Yet I wondered how such a bold thesis would fare under the gaze of the more objective or hard sciences.

As it happened, our little conference was occurring at the same time as a large professional gathering of scientists under the auspices of the Institute for Environmental Studies of the Free University of Amsterdam; and one day it was arranged that our group should visit that consultation. I was astonished at the respect and interest with which James Lovelock was received by the international scientists on that occasion. I believe that his Gaia Theory is still regarded with some skepticism among scientists, but that is not so significant as is the fact that it has stimulated the thinking of many within the scientific community as well as a great many others who reflect deeply on the future of the planet under the impact of human demand, neglect, and contempt.

The above-named booklet did not achieve a wide circulation, but it deserves to be studied at least for its exemplification of profitable dialogue between science and theology today.

That faith, however, must itself be true to the depths of mystery that it confesses. That faith must not devolve into sight, into brave religious pronouncements, into propositions and doctrines and dogmas and ironclad fundamentals. When it does that, it betrays the very Source of wonder to which it is supposed to be bearing witness.

This means that theological modesty is required today, not only where our statements about God—our theologies in the narrower sense—are concerned, but in all things. And the way of negation, at bottom, is nothing more or less than a manner of honoring the mystery of God and the things of God—all the things of God: that is, the heavens and earth and "all creatures great and small," including our own strange and perhaps impossible species.

THE INTENTION OF THIS STUDY

My intention in the chapters that follow, then, is simply to apply that way of negation to the question about Christianity itself. At a time when definitive statements about a religion—any and every religion—are bound to occasion immediate dispute and rejection, may we nevertheless preserve something of the integrity of the Christian faith by trying to identify what it is *not*?

Recently I attended in our university an interesting doctoral oral examination. The basic question of the dissertation being examined was whether the eschatology of Augustine, as presented in his magnum opus, *The City of God*, could have any relevance for feminist theology. It was a good thesis, but an extremely difficult one—more so, I think, than appeared on the surface. As a result, the examiners found themselves frustrated and floundering at many points. Could one, they wondered, legitimately compare a theology developed in the context of fourth-century Rome (already in a state of decay) with theologies emerging out of contemporary Western societies more than a millennium and a half later?

In the final moments of the long examination, the chair or pro-dean of the examining committee, himself a Muslim, was moved to ask, "Are there not perhaps *many* Christianities?"

That was a very perceptive question, and the one that had been begged throughout the discussion. It is also the question that we must ask ourselves here. With a modicum of knowledge of church history, one realizes that Christianity has indeed shown up throughout these twenty-plus centuries in many different forms and guises. And when one encounters Christians from other parts of the world today, one is often struck more by differences than by similarities—differences of spirituality; differences of moral concerns; differences in attitudes toward the Scriptures, church authority, tradition, politics, sexuality, and so forth. Whole Christian denominations are torn apart by such differences. Meetings of ecumenical bodies are often bedeviled by them. Globalization has only increased our knowledge of the bewildering variety of Christian communities and types. Some suggest that the present-day split between Christians of the northern and the southern hemispheres, in this respect, is fraught with more ecclesiastical grief than the Great Schism of East and West in the eleventh century, traditionally dated 1054 CE.[6] Right here on our own continent are diverse and—at least in some cases—wholly incompatible expressions of this ancient faith, all insisting that they are bodying forth Christianity. It is tempting, therefore, as it was for the examiners of that thesis, to conclude that there are simply many Christianities.

But that, it seems to me, is a too-easy way out of what is certainly a dilemma. I am tempted to say that it is in fact an evasion of the problem. Where it is not the product of sheer weariness or indifference (a mood that was certainly observable in the aforementioned doctoral examination!), it courts a numbing relativism and leaves serious Christians in the lurch. Are we to say, simply, that there are all these sorts of Christianity, one as legitimate as the next, so take your pick? Are we ready to give up on the biblical and traditional mark of Christian unity—simply to leave out the word "one" when we repeat marks of the church in the Nicene Creed and elsewhere, and opt for this smorgasbord of Christianities that characterizes the worldwide religious scene today?

I do not wish to imply that Christian unity translates into uniformity. It never has and never will. Indeed, it never *should*! Nor do I wish to suggest that we should, or can, aim for some immutable, permanently true definition of what authentic Christianity is. It seems obvious to me that in the twenty-first century we cannot and should not even attempt to construct binding definitions, in whatever form, of what constitutes true Christianity. Of course many would like to do that, provided their own definitions were the ones accepted! But surely we have learned enough from history to realize that, besides not resolving anything, such regulatory definitions

6. See, e.g., Philip Jenkins, *The Next Christendom: The Coming of Global Christianity* (Oxford: Oxford University Press, 2002).

would only add to the estrangement, suspicion, and violence that already exists among Christians and churches. Few of us are ready for the kinds of excommunications, denunciations, damnations, and burnings at the stake (well, yes—probably that too!) that would prove the logical course of such a procedure.

But neither, on the other hand, can we settle for the status quo, with its plethora of churches and sects and causes and creeds and moralities all claiming to be expressions of Christianity. We cannot rest easy with that existing situation, however we may tolerate it in the meantime, because *some* of these alleged Christianities are dynamite. They are brimful of potentiality for chaos and violence, overflowing with the very stuff out of which "religion kills." Perhaps in an earlier, less volatile age than ours, there was room for the kind of laissez faire that simply left in abeyance the question of truth or legitimacy or authenticity. But we know now that this is not our present situation. In today's world (the world after 9/11, if you wish), what Christians think and do, and do not think or do, matters not only to other Christians but to the whole species—affects indeed the future of the planet. We Christians, who in our heyday as Christendom thought we could control everything, in our humiliated and reduced state are apt to underestimate our own responsibility for the preservation of life. We have become very concerned, many of us, about the Islamic faith, which we feel threatens the planetary future because so much of it seems to have fallen into extremism. Where are the moderate Muslims?, many Christians ask. But Muslims might just as legitimately ask, Where are the moderate and responsible Christians? For in large areas of the Muslim world the Christians, when they do not show up as plain proselytizers, seem the chief spiritual force of imperial Western societies that want to rob Eastern and other peoples of their birthright, and thus foment hostilities.

No, we may not, I think, prescribe what Christianity is and must always be. Even if we could do that, theoretically, it would be a disastrous project, adding untold weight to an already chaotic and potentially lethal religious situation. It would also, of course, be completely impracticable, even absurd. But what we may and can and ought to do, I shall argue here, is to hold up to one another in the churches and to those who care in the world at large some of the ways in which Christianity is being misrepresented and made part of the world's problem, not its redemption, by groups and movements and causes that identify this faith with some of its parts and elements and associations *writ too large*. Perhaps we may no longer speak clearly of the essence of Christianity, as did nineteenth-century theologians and historians like Adolf von Harnack; but surely—humbly, more tentatively, yet with a certain confidence born of faith and historical necessity—we may still have a sufficiently shared sense of the "kerygmatic core" or "heart" of this faith—its *Innerlichkeit*—to be able, in the face of these dangerous misrepresentations of it, to say what it is not.[7]

7. Reluctantly I find myself in some disagreement with what my colleague and friend of many years, the Catholic theologian Gregory Baum, has recently written on this subject:

"Let me first say a few words about the internal pluralism of religious traditions. At one time, scholars believed that it was possible to gain a deep insight into a religion and define its essential characteristics. At the beginning of the twentieth century, Adolf von Harnack, the famous Protestant theologian and historian, published *The Essence of Christianity*; Leo Beck, the learned German rabbi, published *The Essence of Judaism*. Today scholars no longer suppose that religions have an essence. What is recognized today is that religions are produced by communities of interpretation whose faith is based on sacred texts or sacred persons, sources that summon them to worship and guide them in their daily life. Religions are constituted by faith communities that read and reread their sacred texts in the ever-changing circumstances of history. In the search for fidelity to the originating texts or persons, the hermeneutic communities are involved in internal debates and in conversation with the culture in which they dwell. Religions thus have no permanent essence: their identity is created by their effort to remain faithful to the sacred texts. Religions are therefore inevitably marked by an internal pluralism. Each religion has many faces." (Baum, *Signs of the Times: Religious Pluralism and Economic Injustice*[Toronto: Novalis, 2007], 20–21.)

This may be true enough as a description of the religious situation, but apart from its reference to "sacred texts," it does not address the knotty question of authenticity, nor does it leave us with any criteria for recognizing *great distortions* of given religious traditions. One can readily agree that the concept of an essence of a religion evokes the language of another time; nevertheless, the basic inquiry in which Harnack and Beck and others of that age were involved is hardly one that can be abandoned by serious faith and theology. Whether we call it the ongoing quest for the core or kernel or inwardness (*Innerlichkeit*) of the faith, or for contemporary expression of our common heritage, or for a way of articulating the apostolic tradition today, or whatever else, theology—certainly theology in the Christian mode—must constantly attempt to say what belongs to this faith centrally and profoundly, what is peripheral, and what is simply wrongheaded and misleading. The whole task of theology, Christianly conceived, is precisely about that. Without it, Christian intellectual discourse is reduced to history and sociology.

1

Not a Culture-Religion

"Render to Caesar the things that are Caesar's,
and to God the things that are God's"[1]

CHRISTIANITY IS NOT A culture-religion. By that I mean that Christianity is not a religion so inextricably bound up with the history, art, lifestyle, and shared values (culture) of a particular people that it is virtually inseparable from these, and therefore accessible to other cultures only as a total package—e.g., Christianity plus Western culture.[2] I propose that this should be first in our reflections on what Christianity is not, because in this Euro-American context of ours there is a very strong temptation to merge Christianity and our way of life, our culture. All around us there are Christian groupings and Christian voices that regard Christianity as being virtually inseparable from the mores, pursuits, and values that we have come to associate with America. Many of these same voices herald America as the great beacon of Christianity in a dangerously diverse and darkening

1. Jesus, in Mark 2:17 (KJV).

2. Let us acknowledge at once that the word *culture* is a confusing term. It is confusing because particularly from the eighteenth century onwards it has been used in at least three different ways—to mean: 1) the acquisition of sophistication in the arts and humanities (*They are a cultured family*); 2) a comprehensive and integrated system of belief and behavior (*the culture of Athens*); 3) a way of life, composed of memories, habits, religious assumptions and practices, social conventions, languages, arts, and the like, shared by a group such as a country, organization, extended family, and so forth. It is the third sense in which I shall use the term *culture* in this chapter; it would be a total misunderstanding of the argument of this chapter, therefore, to interpret it as meaning that Christianity is opposed to culture in the first or second senses above.

world. Even those of us who try to convey a more nuanced view of the relation between Christianity and our particular culture are tempted often to gauge the course of Christianity in the world by its status within own society, to the point of our being—in our churches—constantly at work amassing statistics and number crunching.

This tendency of North American Christians to meld Christianity and our culture is not new. Sidney Mead, who was widely regarded as the dean of American church historians, wrote of the Americanization of Christianity—especially Protestantism. He maintained that from the middle of the nineteenth century the practice of using the terms *Protestantism* and *Americanism* almost synonymously became very common.[3] In some circles, one might argue, this practice is still more pronounced today, or at least it is pursued more aggressively. For with the advent of widespread multiculturalism and religious pluralism, as well as our society's post-9/11 apprehension of militant Islam, the mindset that finds an indelible association between the Christian religion and America has become increasingly insistent and defensive. A narrative has emerged in which the actual variety of religious influences that characterized America's beginnings, including not only Unitarianism and Deism but also secular humanism, tends to be forgotten, and is replaced by an ultra-evangelicalism and biblicism that would hardly have been applauded by Jefferson, Franklin, John A. MacDonald (the first prime minister of Canada), and other architects of this society.

Now, obviously enough, Christianity can never be extricated entirely from its social and historical matrix; and undoubtedly it will happen that the more quantitatively successful and politically influential a religion becomes, the more transparently will its host society reflect that religion, or at least its more prominent public aspects. But even in a highly Christianized society—hypothetically, even in a monolithically Christian society—should it not remain possible for thoughtful Christians to distinguish between their faith and its cultural environs, its social wrappings? Ancient Israel could and often did boast that it was unshakably loyal to the monotheistic principles of the Mosaic faith: "We have Abraham as our father," cried John the Baptist's Pharisaic and other critics (e.g., Luke 3:8). But this claim prevented neither the Baptist nor Jesus nor the prophets before them from engaging in a relentless and often brutally critical denunciation of Israel's

---

3. Sidney Mead, *The Lively Experiment: The Shaping of Christianity in America* (New York: Harper & Row, 1963), 134.

presumption and virtual apostasy. It is in fact this ancient paradigm of the distinction between religion and prophetic faith on which I shall draw for the main substance of this chapter and, indeed, this study as a whole.

But first we must pause long enough to pay attention to a point—a biblical point much neglected today—even more radical than the insistence that Christianity is not a culture-religion. And that is that Christianity is *not a religion, period.*

NOT A RELIGION!

If we take the Bible to be the primary witness to the heart and core of this faith (and in the tradition of classical Protestantism that is certainly what we should do), we must realize that this collection of writings, accumulated over a period of a thousand years, contains an extraordinarily consistent and often intense quarrel with religion. The prophets of the older Testament waged a continuing struggle against religion, both outside and (even more vehemently) inside their own religious community.

> I hate, I despise your festivals
>   and I take no delight in your solemn assemblies . . .
> Take away from me the noise of your songs;
> I will not listen to the melody of your harps.
> But let justice role down like waters . . . (Amos 5:21–22, RSV)

The bitterest opponents of Jesus, and the ones he himself frequently singled out for censor, were those regarded by his society as being the most religious of all. Jesus's quarrel with the scribes and Pharisees has nothing to do with their being Jewish—that is a vicious fiction of later interpreters, perhaps already beginning with certain strains in the New Testament itself. Jesus himself was Jewish (Christians cannot say that too often!). His criticism of these superreligious ones (criticism strictly in line with the whole prophetic tradition of Israel) rather is at base a criticism of the characteristic tendencies of religion as such, especially when it has hardened into dogma and ritual and moral codes and is made the acid test of human worth and belonging.

"The message of the Bible," the young Karl Barth was moved to say (because, as minister in a Swiss village that loved to think itself impeccably religious, he knew all about Protestant smugness!) "is that God hates religion." What we must say about religion, Barth writes, is "that it is the one great concern of *godless* man."[4] Barth included in his voluminous *Church Dogmatics* a whole section (about thirty long pages of small print!) titled "Religion as Unbelief"[5]—a piece of theological reflection comparable to Kierkegaard's *Attack upon Christendom*. Religion, Barth wrote—

> is a *grasping* . . . [M]an [*sic*!] tries to grasp at truth [by] himself . . . But in that case he does not do what he has to do when the truth comes to him. He does not *believe*. If he did, he would listen; but in religion he talks. If he did, he would accept a gift; but in religion he takes something for himself. If he did, he would let God Himself intercede for God; but in religion he ventures to grasp at God.[6]

Paul Tillich, though he often disagreed with Barth, was very close to the Swiss theologian in this warning about the wiles of religion. In a sermon titled "The Yoke of Religion," based on the Scripture text, "Come unto me, all ye that labor and are heavy laden . . . take *my* yoke upon you," (Matthew 11:28, KJV), Tillich argues that the burden Jesus wants to take from us is "the burden of religion." He continues:

> We are all permanently in danger of abusing Jesus by stating that He is the founder of a new religion, and the bringer of another, more refined, and more enslaving law. And so we see in all Christian Churches the toiling and labouring of people who are called Christians, serious Christians, under innumerable laws which they cannot fulfill, from which they flee, to which they return, or which they replace by other laws. This is the yoke from which Jesus wants to liberate us. He is more than a priest or a prophet or a religious genius. These all subject us to religion. He frees us from religion. They make new religious laws; He overcomes the religious law . . .
>
> We call Jesus the Christ not because He brought a new religion, but because He is the end of religion, above religion and irreligion, above Christianity and non-Christianity. We spread his call because it is the call to every [person] in every period to receive the New Being, that hidden saving power in our existence, which takes from us labor and burden, and gives rest to our souls.[7]

It is true that Tillich, elsewhere, is able to use the term *religion* in a more neutral or sometimes even a positive way, namely, as human striving

4. *Church Dogmatics* I/2, trans. G. T. Thomson and Harold Knight (Edinburgh: T. & T. Clark, 1956), 300.

5. Ibid. 297–325.

6. Ibid., 302.

7. Tillich, *The Shaking of the Foundations* (London: SCM, 1949), 93ff.

for meaning and deliverance to which the revelation in Christ comes as answer. But the answer—the gospel or (as he more often calls it) "the Christian message"—is at the same time an answer to the quest of religion and a critique of that quest. Like Barth and most others belonging to the great renewal of Protestant theology in the first half of the twentieth century that is called (not very instructively) neo-orthodoxy,[8] Tillich finds religion at best ambiguous and at worst (as in this sermon) a terrible "burden" under which humankind labors.

Indeed, this kind of distinction between faith and religion became one of twentieth-century Protestantism's most important insights. One wonders today, when in our many university departments of religion we have so much to say on the subject, whatever happened to this critique of the whole phenomenon! Dietrich Bonhoeffer was another who frequently drew upon this critique and the need to differentiate religion from faith. Bonhoeffer acknowledged that Karl Barth was "the first theologian to begin the criticism of religion—and that [he said] remains his really great merit."[9] Religion, Bonhoeffer believed, is not at all what Christianity at its kerygmatic core is about. "Jesus," he writes, "does not call [people] to a new religion, but to *life*."[10] Following an exegetical tradition dating back to the early church, he contrasts the account of Pentecost in the second chapter of Acts with the myth of the Tower of Babel in Genesis 11. Babel is the Bible's most dramatic symbolic depiction of the religious impulse—the impulse, as Barth called it, of "grasping" after the ultimate, the struggle for possession and *securitas*. In that myth, it will be remembered, human beings, terrified by the precariousness of their creaturehood (well, human creaturehood *is* precarious; the Bible does not make light of that!), reach up after divine transcendence in a pathetic yet futile effort to secure the future. Their absurd tower—the prototype of many towers!—is an attempt, as it were, to get hold of and control the Controller. What they get instead is a still greater consciousness of their finitude and vulnerability: intent upon possessing divinity, they end in an even greater failure of humanity. Their communality is destroyed, and they cannot communicate with one another any longer. By contrast, Bonhoeffer saw, Pentecost, the beginnings of the Christian movement, does not depict

---

8. See Hall, *Remembered Voices: Reclaiming the Legacy of "Neo-Orthodoxy"* (Louisville: Westminster John Knox, 1998).

9. Bonhoeffer, *Letters and Papers from Prison*, trans. Reginald Fuller (London: SCM, 1953), 126.

10. Ibid., 167 (italics added).

human beings grasping after the Absolute but the reverse: it depicts the Spirit of God grasping and transforming human beings. Babel, the religious quest, ends in greater human alienation; Pentecost, the birth of faith, effects reconciliation among those, even, who cannot fully understand one another.[11]

Why, we may ask, is it important for us today to revisit and reclaim this neo-orthodox critique of religion—not just of culture-religion, but of religion as such? In the first place, I would say, we should do so because the critique is not just a twentieth-century theological invention but a courageous attempt to recover a genuine and unavoidable *biblical* theme—a biblical theme marginalized and lost sight of, for the most part, as soon as the Christian religion took upon itself the role of religious establishment. A religion that wants to incorporate and commend itself to everyone cannot afford to be self-critical. It must be promotional, upbeat, positive! During the Christendom ages, whenever biblical texts arose critical of religion, such as those famous lines of Amos about God's hatred of cultic worship, it could be (and was) explained that such denunciations applied not to the church but to the synagogue—that is, to the failed parental faith that Christianity was destined to displace and replace! The critique of religion is genuine, however, only when the community of faith knows that this critique applies to itself—that this is part of "the judgment [that] begins with the household of God" (1 Peter 4:17).

But there is an even more important reason why this biblical and neo-orthodox critique of religion needs to be studied and reflected upon today, as part of our attempt, as Christians, to discover a way of living responsibly in the midst of a religiously pluralistic civilization. If and insofar as religion is inherently a kind of grasping, as Barth insisted, it follows that the religious impulse will also be inherently competitive and conflictual. A spiritual struggle motivated by the desire for permanence, certitude, and the possession of ultimate power and verity is not likely to manifest much openness to other claims to truth. To the contrary, it will in all likelihood

---

11. See e.g. Bonhoeffer's letter to his parents on Ascension Day, June 4, 1943 (ibid.); but there are allusions to these texts in various writings of the martyr.

Bonhoeffer's critique of religion goes even farther in his final writings, where he speaks of the prospect of a "religionless Christianity" or "non-religious Christianity," in which faith is liberated from the confines of the "religious consciousness" in which it has been "soaked." See the writings of Bonhoeffer in *Letters and Papers* for May and June of 1944. See also the discussion of this subject in Larry Rasmussen with Renate Bethge, *Dietrich Bonhoeffer: His Significance for North Americans* (Minneapolis: Fortress, 1992), esp. 6off.

manifest the kind of exclusiveness that guards its spiritual treasures zealously, and, having as it thinks wrested them from eternity, claims sole ownership of them. Its attitude will be some version of a pronouncement I heard recently from a true-believing Christian reflecting upon Islam: "If I'm right, they're wrong." But who can say "I'm right" with that kind of unwavering certitude? Who, *coram Deo*—standing in the presence of the living God—can attribute such finality to his or her own religious claims?

In introducing this study, I suggested that in all religions there are vulnerable spots—ideas, attitudes, or emphases that under certain socio-historical conditions are bound to become flash points of conflict. But what we must conclude on the basis of the above analysis is that, at bottom, it is religion itself and as such that constitutes the greatest and most permanent point of friction. Since it concerns that which a community regards as ultimate, the religion of one culture is bound to look upon the religions of other cultures with suspicion and mistrust. In a global village where religious disputation no longer limits itself to quarrels within Christendom but spills over increasingly into the unprecedented meeting of world religions, all of them made newly insecure by their new proximity to and consciousness of one another, the greatest flash point of all is inseparable from the religious impulse as such; with its grasping after security, its scramble for the absolute, and its incapacity for self-doubt and dialogue with others, religion in the global village seems destined for a history of violence. The newly popular atheism of today understands this and capitalizes on it. It argues, with a kind of dogged logic, that the only way humankind can avoid the great catastrophes to which this situation points is by dispensing altogether with "the God delusion." But Christians are called to embrace a greater realism than that! No one—and certainly not a bevy of smugly atheistic intellectuals—is going to rid *homo sapiens* of the religious impulse. Contrary to Bonhoeffer's late musings about the disappearance of *homo religiosus*,[12] it seems likely that human beings will continue to build their towers of Babel, world without end. Sometimes, perhaps especially in times of great insecurity, the religious quest will be dominant; at other times it will be weak or even peripheral. Sometimes it will be religious in the traditional sense; at other times it will be some secular ideology dressed up in what are essentially religious pretentions to finality. But Christians who consider the biblical critique of religion and the role of the Christ in relation to it will be able at least to maintain a critical perspective on religion—especially their

---

12. That is, the belief that humans are by nature religious.

own Christian religion! They will be delivered a little, as Tillich says, from the "burden" of religion, which is religion's perennial temptation to take heaven by storm, to imagine itself above mere creaturehood, and to award itself the place of ultimacy.

And this critical perspective, this distancing ourselves from true-believing religion, is not only the condition without which there can be no significant interfaith dialogue, it is the condition without which the peace of the world from now on will never be sustained. Certainly we must meet one another, in this great new parliament of global religions, as persons of faith; but faith is not synonymous with religion. Probably faith never will be found apart from religion, some religion; but the biblically and theologically informed Christian will nevertheless be able to distinguish between what comes of faith and what comes of religion. And the greatest distinction of all, in this contrast, lies in the readiness of faith, unlike religion, to confess its incompleteness and insufficiency. By definition, faith is a deficiency, a lack, a not seeing (1 Corinthians 13:12), a longing that is made even more poignant by the fact that it *is*—tentatively, expectantly—in touch with the Ultimate. Authentic faith can never rest content with itself; it can never extinguish its own existential antithesis, doubt; it can never feel that it has arrived at its destination—that now it sees face to face and no longer "through a glass darkly."

Listen to the way faith speaks, in a statement by one of the great Christian activists and lay theologians of our epoch, a French Protestant who was part of the Resistance, and who was so committed to the possibility of the reign of God that he did not stop with resistance but became the mayor of Bordeaux, thus demonstrating the Reformation insistence that true faith begets (as well as modesty) the courage to work for change. His name was Jacques Ellul, and this is how he described faith:

> Faith is a terribly caustic substance, a burning acid. It puts to the test every element of my life and society; it spares nothing. It leads me ineluctably to question my certitudes, all my moralities, beliefs and policies. It forbids me to attach ultimate significance to any expression of human activity. It detaches and delivers me from money and the family, from my job and my knowledge. It's the surest road to realizing that 'the only thing I know is that I don't know anything.'[13]

13. Ellul, *Living Faith: Belief and Doubt in a Perilous World*, trans. Peter Heinegg (San Francisco: Harper & Row, 1983), 111.

Such faith, and not religion, is the prerequisite for dialogue between the religions today; and such dialogue is the prerequisite for civilization's survival.

CULTURE-RELIGION AND PROPHETIC FAITH

This distinction between faith and religion, which (as I've noted) was one of the most important insights of the neo-orthodox school, always prevents me from saying straightforwardly, as people do in ordinary discourse, that Christianity is a religion. In its essence, at its kerygmatic heart—that is, *as gospel*—it is not. As Barth, Tillich, Bonhoeffer, and many others have insisted, Jesus did not come to add yet another religion to the world's already exhaustive and exhausting religious agenda!

But of course in its historical pilgrimage Christianity has been, is universally described as being, and still even thinks of itself as . . . a religion: a religion that may be compared with other religions; a religion that itself bears all the earmarks of the religions grasping that the Bible and the most faithful theology call in question. As I have already suggested, it is in fact doubtful that one could find *any* instance or exemplification of Christianity, now or in the past, that did not combine in subtle and confusing ways Pentecost and Babel, faith and religion; and in all likelihood most of what has been called Christianity and continues to be designated such has more of Babel than of Pentecost in it! All the same, it is necessary for serious Christians to keep the *distinction* between faith and religion always in mind, and to apply it in very concrete and practical ways in the daily life of the church. Empirically speaking, Christianity may never be found apart from a combination of these two antithetical movements of the human spirit—grasping and being grasped, reaching after the absolute and being encountered by the unreachable absolute. But the Christian community that has lost the capacity intellectually and spiritually to distinguish the two at the level of thought and language will be a community in danger of losing its soul.

An important way in which theological scholars during the past century have tried to preserve this distinction is by contrasting two types of religion: culture-religion and prophetic religion. If we are to use the term *religion* at all to describe Christianity, I believe that something like that type of contrast must be maintained. It may be too daring—and for many too confusing—to say straightforwardly that Christianity is not a religion. But at least contemporary Christians should try to comprehend what it means when theologians insist that at its revelatory core, Christianity is not and ought not to be practiced as a '*culture*-religion.'

The term *culture-religion* came into prominence in North America in the 1960s, though its antecedents—particularly in German theologies—are much earlier. The term has a particular usefulness in our New World setting, where (as I claimed at the beginning of this chapter) there is a continuing tendency to merge 'Christ and Culture' (to use the well-known categories of H. Richard Niebuhr).[14]

Christianity in the United States and Canada was never established *legally*, as it was in the European motherlands, though attempts at legal establishment were made here too; but, instead, what occurred on this continent—more as a matter of habit and association than as anything planned—was the gradual but effective identification of our culture or way of life with the Christian faith. We learned to consider ourselves Christian societies and Christian nations, and to equate Christianity more or less with what we have built here—our way of governing ourselves, our moral codes, our values.

For reasons that many of us are still trying to decipher, this tendency to equate religion and culture was always more prevalent in US-American experience than in the northern country of the continent, Canada. There has always been, I think, a stubborn streak of skepticism in the Canadian spirit, as there is in the spirit of most northern peoples (the Scandinavians and the Scots, for example): it's hard to believe in God and all that when it's so cold, and you're living on a rock like the Canadian (Precambrian) Shield! The United States inherited not only a more hospitable terrain but a much heavier dose of Modern optimism, and its Christianity evolved accordingly. I think what surprises many Canadians and Europeans about church life in the United States (sometimes it charms them, sometimes they just find it excessive) is the combination of rather simplistic theology and rather stringent morality with enthusiastic and exaggerated displays of happiness, or what passes for happiness. There is a celebratory ring in most worship in US-American settings that neither Canadians nor Europeans can duplicate. When we try to do so, the results are usually quite laughable. The celebratory spirit of US religion cannot be imitated in other social contexts because its secret is its combination of religious piety and cultural complacency. It is a celebration of the culture, including its economic success and

14. H. Richard Niebuhr, *Christ and Culture* (New York: Harper, 1951).

political preeminence, at least as much as it is a celebration of the religion that contributed so much to the shaping of the culture.

Peter L. Berger, whose book *The Noise of Solemn Assemblies* was a kind of milestone in the Anglo-Saxon deployment of the term *culture-religion*, explained this type of equation in the following way:

> American society possesses a cultural religion that is vaguely de-rived from the Judaeo-Christian tradition and that contains values generally held by most Americans. The cultural religion gives sol-emn ratification to these values. The cultural religion is politically established on all levels of government, receiving from the state both moral and economic support. The religious denominations, whatever else they may believe or practice, are carriers of this cultural religion. Affiliation with a religious denomination thus becomes *ipso facto* an act of allegiance to the common political creed. Disaffiliation, in turn, renders an individual not only reli-giously but also politically suspect.[15]

Why is such an identification of Christianity and culture theologically problematic? What price does the Christian movement pay for this kind of proximity to the dominant culture? As a way into my answer to that ques-tion, I want to quote a sentence of Reinhold Niebuhr—it is in fact the very first sentence of Niebuhr's 1935 book, *An Interpretation of Christian Eth-ics*: "Protestant Christianity in America," it runs, "is, unfortunately, unduly dependent upon the very culture of modernity, the disintegration of which would offer a more independent religion a unique opportunity."[16]

In this one sentence, Niebuhr puts his finger precisely on the conse-quences of practicing Christianity as a culture-religion. By allowing itself to be absorbed by the evolving culture, the Christian faith loses its poten-tiality for being responsible in and to and for that culture—for being, in biblical terms, salt, yeast, and light in its social context. It forfeits this *pro-phetic* calling for the sake of the shallow kind of acceptance and popularity and quantitative success that it may acquire through its accommodation of itself to the governing spirit of its host society. It has little or nothing beyond rhetoric to bring to that society distinguishable from the society's existing assumptions and experiences; and this is particularly conspicu-ous and unfortunate when, in situations of social crisis, the society needs

15. Berger, *The Noise of Solemn Assemblies: Christian Commitment and the Religious Establishment in America* (Garden City, NY: Doubleday, 1961), 63.

16. Reinhold Niebuhr, *An Interpretation of Christian Ethics* (New York: Harper, 1935), 3.

precisely some light from beyond its own resources—needs to hear, precisely, a voice that does not simply echo its own tired and failed ambitions, its Babel confusion. The ending of modernity, of which (in this perceptive sentence) Reinhold Niebuhr spoke decades before anyone heard the word *postmodern*—the end and crisis of modernity creates for prophetic faith an "opportunity" that faith communities rarely have when societies are in their heyday: an opportunity (one must say in Niebuhr's behalf), not to enhance their membership roles and social standing, but to speak truthfully, to act out of genuine hope and not just social optimism, to enhance and preserve the life—the life not of the church but of the world to which the church is sent. Because most Protestantism in America had given itself so unconditionally to the modern vision, Niebuhr believed, it was not in a position to offer any alternative vision at the point when modernity began to show how shallow, deceptive, and dangerous a vision it was.

Stating the point in other language, culture-religion lacks the necessary distance from its host society to be truly responsible in and for that society. It is so much *of* its world that it has nothing distinctive to bring *to* its world, only more of the same—undoubtedly in stained-glass accents. In the end, while it may perform a certain pastoral and ritual function among people, Christianity as culture-religion serves more conspicuously those powers that have their own self-enhancing designs upon society: powers that benefit from the status quo and are therefore very glad to support a religion that helps to maintain the status quo.

Now, while culture-religion has a particular application to Christianity in America, it is by no means a new phenomenon. It is just a modern version of the very ancient idea and reality of religious establishment. It is an adaptation of this idea undertaken in more or less democratic societies where decisions about religion cannot be ordered from the top down, as was the case in Europe from Constantine onwards. It describes the *kind* of establishment that was worked out in this New World setting, a setting that positively rejected and despised the Old World versions of Christian establishment (since most of our pioneer forebears were fleeing precisely from those legal establishments of old Europe), but a setting that at the same time was not ready to entertain the idea of religious *disestablishment*. With some important exceptions, we seem incapable of entertaining the thought of Christian disestablishment to this very day. The concept of the separation of church and state is perhaps a polite bow in that direction, but it is also very deceptive, because the establishment we fashioned on this continent was never a de jure (legal or formal) one such as an agreement with the state would usually be, but a de facto informal relationship with the culture at large. Maintaining the separation of church and *state* (which itself often proves to be more rhetorical than real) does little to affect a distinction between Christianity and *culture*. That distinction can only be maintained at the level of the church's theology, preaching, and public witness.

Why are we so steadfastly committed to the idea of Christian establishment? Our forebears said no to legal establishment, and we can be glad of that; but why should Christians seek establishment of any kind? Is there anything in the Christian gospel that would lead us in that direction? To the contrary, as Kierkegaard insisted, is there not in the gospel of the cross that which would deny Christians such a comfortable relationship with the world? Yet despite the biblical warnings against it, the notion that Christianity is quite naturally and properly a religion bound to seek some form of establishment—including some special relationship with the policy-making classes and governing institutions, but more important (in democratic societies) the achievement of majority status and people power—this notion is such a hoary one, itself so entrenched in church history and popular Christian imagination that it is terribly hard to displace or even to critique it. After all, it has been around for at least fifteen or sixteen centuries, by far the greater share of Christian history. It is assumed—most Christians in the United States (and many in Canada), I suspect, simply assume—that the very *mission* of the church is to achieve establishment in some form or other, if only by being able to claim greater numbers than other power groupings; it is also assumed that churches and Christians who do not manifest that aim, or who may even be very critical of it, are simply failing as missional communities. Again and again the great commission of Matthew's gospel[17] is cited to lend biblical weight to the belief that Christianity is positively intended for majority status, that is, for establishment, ergo that something has gone radically wrong when churches experience quantitative losses or an apparent loss of popular support.

Within the past few decades, however, and particularly in the aftermath of the brief and rather disillusioning run on the mainline churches that occurred in the 1950s, more and more people within the once most established churches in North America and elsewhere began to notice

17. Matthew 28:19-20 (RSV), according to which the risen Christ commands his disciples to "Go therefore and make disciples of all nations, baptizing them in the name of the Father and of the Son and of the Holy Spirit, and teaching them to obey everything that I have commanded you . . ."

some of the flaws of establishment religion. Today significant minorities in all the American and Canadian old-line denominations not only question the role of Christianity as a culture-religion but have sufficiently distanced themselves from the dominant culture so that they are frequently accused by self-declared conservative Christians of betraying both Christianity and their nation. Perhaps the most astonishing aspect of contemporary life in North America is that so many Christians in denominations that were until about 1960 the most culturally established of all have given various kinds of indication that they believe Christianity is fundamentally at loggerheads with our way of life. The nearly unanimous protest against the wars in Iraq and Afghanistan on the part of the once-mainline churches of the United States and Canada is only one indicator of this new situation. I myself have lived long enough to observe my own denomination, the United Church of Canada, morph from being, certainly, the most culturally established Protestant church in Canada to achieving a countrywide reputation for radicalism and conspicuous divergence from the historical norms and counsels of conventional religion in our country. Even persons in these old denominations who lament the passing of social prestige and respectability have, most of them, been caused to wonder whether Christianity may not be—in its *essence*—something quite different from what it has usually been. As Sallie McFague writes, "Wiggle as we will, most of us North American comfortable mainline Christians know there is probably something wrong with a Christian faith that does not involve a countercultural stance."[18]

Perhaps just at this point, however, a parenthesis is required; for the mention of *countercultural* approaches to Christian faith and mission introduces another question, which critics of the Christian Left do not fail to belabor: Is there not a danger in some ecclesiastical circles that the Christian religion will be uncritically allied with certain *countercultural* ideologies, identities, and causes? Is it not possible for Christians who are critical of the dominant culture to pursue uncritical identity with counter- or alternative cultures, and is this tendency perhaps just as questionable from the perspective of prophetic faith as the older approach? When the church leaps from association with the establishment to greater solidarity with anti-establishment forces and factions, is it not in danger of seeking legitimization through association with the protesting minority, and thus

---

18. McFague, *Life Abundant: Rethinking Theology and Economy for a Planet in Peril* (Minneapolis: Fortress, 2001), 34.

of manifesting once again the same old lack of courage to stand alone—by faith alone?

It would be wrong, I think, to dismiss this critique out of hand. Sometimes what we may call *the habit of establishment* manifests itself in quests for proximity to protesting minorities on the part of Christians who are disillusioned with the cultural majority. It is no solution of the dangers of establishment when Christians move from an unexamined conventional identification with established power to an easy endorsement of movements of protest against that power. It may be quite justifiable when the *Christian* protest aligns itself with other forms of social protest; but it remains true that Christians must always try to be quite clear about their own inherent reasons for protest. That is to say, *theological* reflection is always required of the church. It is not enough to assume that every cause that announces its espousal of justice, peace, and the integrity of creation can without further ado be embraced by Christians.

One must speak of this openly, for there is a certain danger among ultraliberal or self-consciously radical elements in the once mainline churches that countercultural solidarity with this or that social protest will be thought natural, right, and good *without any further theological reflection.* The fact of protesting seems in these circles to justify the stance. There is a tendency here, not unconnected with the thrill of protest in itself, to seek Christian authentication through endorsement by popular countercultural causes and identities. As Christians, we have our own reasons for being ecologically, racially, sexually, aesthetically, and in other ways vigilant and involved in today's changing social scene. We do not have to borrow from others a rationale for environmental stewardship or for concern over marginalized groups or for international economic justice or for world peace. We have an ancient, profound, tried-and-true tradition of ontological and ethical wisdom upon which to draw; and wherever Christian groups have drawn upon that wisdom faithfully and with imagination, they have not only brought an independent voice to the chorus of those who struggle for greater humanity in the earth; they have been welcomed by others because they could contribute insight and perspective often lacking in other protesting groups. We need not be ashamed of the tradition that makes our prophetic protest possible. We need not turn elsewhere to find authentication.

Having introduced this topic parenthetically, however, I certainly do not want to overemphasize the need to maintain a little critical distance in our relationships with countercultural elements in our present society. One of the most hopeful aspects of today's chaotic world is that as Christians we may quite legitimately make common cause with so many others who are concerned for the future of the planet and human civilization. Ours is a time of experimentation: old relationships are perhaps no longer reliable; new relationships may be possible and productive. George A. Lindbeck has named this period in the history of Christianity an "awkward intermediate stage": we are moving (he says) from a position of "having once been culturally established" to one in which we are "not yet clearly disestablished."[19] In this interim it is, I think, inevitable that the most serious Christians and Christian groupings will experiment with all kinds of new arrangements and alliances. Some of these will prove unhelpful or wrong, and some will be or become important—will prove a way into the future. I think we should try to see in all such experiments, as in the mostly unorganized dissatisfaction with the so-called Christian cultural establishment that is their background, a certain continuity with what has been best in Christianity throughout the ages, and was of the very essence of the Protestant Reformation. "The most important contribution of Protestantism to the world in the past, present and future," wrote Tillich in 1948, "is the principle of prophetic protest against every power which claims divine character for itself—whether it be church or state, party or leader." And we could echo, with emphasis, Tillich's next sentence: "this prophetic, Protestant protest is more necessary today than at any time since the period of the Reformation."[20]

That protest, which Tillich never limited (nor should we) to Protestants, is more needful today than ever because the *religious* divisions into which the planet has fallen are, as we have seen, arguably the most dangerous of all the threats to planetary future, providing as they do the spiritual impetus and emotional fervor for our various types of enmity and warfare. And so long as Christianity is equated in the minds of most of the world's peoples with Western Christendom or simply the West or Western civilization or the Western imperialism that is centered in the most avowedly Christian country of our hemisphere, Christianity will not contribute to the hope of the world but to its despair. Nothing is more needful for all Christians of insight and goodwill today, whether leaders or led, than to

19. Lindbeck, *The Nature of Doctrine: Religion and Theology in a Post-Liberal Age* (Philadelphia: Westminster, 1984), 134.

20. Tillich, *The Protestant Era* (Chicago: University of Chicago Press, 1948), 230.

distance this faith from all the imperial baggage that it has picked up in its long historical pilgrimage and still carries about—often, alas, boastfully. Whatever Christianity *has been* and in many ways still is empirically, at its kerygmatic core, it is not and was never meant to be a culture-religion. And its reputation for being such, however deeply entrenched in history and in the minds and hearts of all of us must be countered from now on by a determination on the part of serious Christians to open this faith to a new *planetary* consciousness that transcends the racial, ethnic, gender, sexual, economic, and political specificity that has shaped our Christendom past.

CHRISTIANITY AND CULTURAL/RELIGIOUS DIVERSITY

Throughout the West today Christians find themselves surrounded by others who are "not of this [Christian] fold."[21] This situation is particularly noticeable in Western Europe (England, France, Germany et al.). In Canada, which has adopted multiculturalism officially and legally, and where (with few exceptions) the churches are quite obviously in decline, the realities of the new multicultural context often seem overwhelming to Christians who belong to the original ethnic and denominational groupings.[22] Like the European nations from which most of our founding families came, we Canadians have been conditioned to assume that our nation and society is at base Christian. Now, quite suddenly, really, we find ourselves one element within a multiculture, one religion in the midst of a plurality of religions faiths. Indeed, as do the older, historically Christian nations of Europe, we often feel we are being pushed out of the center of a stage that we had come to consider our own. Nor does it help that our highly ambitious, innovative, and efficient Western Christian societies, precisely because of

21. Interestingly, in his relatively long discourse on the metaphor of sheep, St John's Jesus introduces the quite radical idea that as Shepherd of the sheep who know his voice (the disciple community), he has "other sheep that do not belong to this fold" (10:16, NRSV). It is a direct—and to many alarming!—critique of the kind of exclusivity that refuses to look beyond the confines of the acknowledged community of belief.

22. In many ways, I think, the Canadian situation is a better gauge of the Christian future than is the United States. In US-America, Christianity in its multitudinous forms has played a *political* role, upon which politicians (especially of the Right) constantly draw. The sociological status of Christianity in the large cities of America, especially but not only in the northern states, indicates that this use of evangelical and fundamentalist forms of Christianity has a limited lifespan. Rampant secularity and religious plurality will undoubtedly color the American scene increasingly with the passage of time.

their material successes, have spawned resentment and mistrust in other societies that have been exploited or ignored by our capitalist-technological rush to preeminence. Heretofore, only a few of the more urbane citizens of Western nations have noticed the depths of this resentment and anger; but now there are living among us—right next door, often—immigrants from these less developed societies who, many of them, are no longer prepared to honor, silently, the historical and numerical dominance of *our* culture, but remind us again and again that Canada is now, after all, *an officially multi-cultural society* so that no one culture, ethnic, linguistic, or religious group should be favored—*no matter how long it has held sway on these shores.* "We are all immigrants," it is said. "Everyone has the right to a place under this sun!"

It is hardly necessary to document the fact that this has created certain lingering tensions among us. Should we tolerate the infighting that other groups have brought to these shores from their long histories of revenge? Should everyone, regardless of their contribution to the democratic institutions that have undoubtedly attracted so many to this country in the first place, be permitted to draw upon privileges and rights and sources of aid that have been centuries in the making? Although we are admittedly a *post*-Christian society, our values and mores, as well as our institutions, have been profoundly influenced by historic Christianity. To what extent, in that case, can we accept into our public life customs and moral practices born of other religious traditions, which clearly go against the grain of our common lifestyle or culture? How extensively are we obliged by our official multiculturalism to *accommodate*—to make room for "exotic" religious practices, conspicuously different moral codes, unusual modes of attire, and so forth? Recently in eastern Canada we have witnessed the long courtroom drama of a family, three members of which appear to have murdered four other (not incidentally, female!) members in a so-called honor killing. How far can divergences go before they are rejected as unacceptable—or even heinous (a term that one heard frequently in the discourse surrounding this so-called honor killing)?

It is obvious—and it is somehow understandable—that the older, established citizenry feel defensive in these circumstances. They feel often that they are no longer quite welcome in their own homeland; that they dare not raise their voices in protest, because if they are not found actually to be breaking the law, they may certainly hear it said of them that they are racists or bigots, or at least grossly inhospitable to strangers—in effect, that they are un-Canadian!

Not infrequently, in their self-defense members of established groups draw upon their religious heritage—even when they themselves no longer practice the faith in which they were reared (which is frequently the case in our highly secularized country). Those of us who are believing Christians or serious about our faith (yes, we too) are tempted to complain, in the face of actions and events that seem to us strange, bizarre, or even shocking, that such behavior is totally incompatible with our way of life, with our Christian faith!

We have here, thus, a situation that is making demands of us as Christians that have never been made heretofore on such a large scale. We are in fact confronted by a very practical—even an excruciating—exemplification of the principal question discussed in this chapter: *If it is true that Christianity is not a culture-religion, how shall we distinguish what is truly Christian from what is (perhaps quite inconspicuously) cultural accretion?*

There are, I suggest, two necessary stages in any serious attempt to respond to this question. The first stage, which is absolutely vital, has to do with the basic perspective and attitude brought to the question. The main alternatives here can best be described by applying the distinction between religion and faith, which has been the central theme of this chapter. So long as Christians come to this question as *religious* persons, concerned for the preservation, rectitude, and dominance of the Christian religion and the culture with which it is allied, they will in all likelihood find the multiculture uncomfortable, to say the least, and probably quite unacceptable. Christendom does not easily or readily admit of alternatives! To encounter the multiculture from the perspective of *faith*, on the other hand, is to do so first of all in a spirit of *modesty*. For faith knows that it is not sight. Faith realizes that the whole substance of one's belief falls infinitely far short of the splendor, the *gloria Dei*, that it glimpses now and then, here and there. One need not abandon one's belief or keep it hidden under a bushel of bourgeois niceness; but one remembers that one's belief, one's theology, is indeed a matter of *faith*, and so one is appropriately humble and respectful in one's converse with others whose beliefs are quite different.

Such a posture may appear strange and even cowardly to Christians who assume a certain entitlement to evangelical boldness. That assumption is the consequence of fifteen or sixteen centuries of Christian hegemony. But if we consider Christian beginnings and the manner in which the pre-Constantinian church went about its mission, we are shown quite another way of being "ambassadors for Christ" (2 Corinthians 5:20, NRSV). It should not be forgotten, as we move into the terra incognita of the post-Christendom future, that the early church lived under conditions very similar to our own. The church that we meet in the New Testament's Gospels and Epistles is a church whose social context is, if anything, even more multicultural and religiously pluralistic than is ours. At no time prior to the Constantinian–Theodosian establishment of Christianity did Christians count for more than, at most, 10 percent of the population of the Roman empire. The New Testament Gospels and Epistles were written under these social conditions—*not* under the conditions of Christendom! Christians in the early church learned courage, but they also learned modesty—to the point of adopting secret signs like the fish,[23] through which they could know one another. For the most part, they moved about among Jews and among worshipers of the old gods of Greece and Rome and soothsayers and believers in magic, and skeptics—just as we today must do, *mutatis mutandis.* These early Christians (some, of course, more than others) learned as well a certain theological and evangelical propriety. When asked, or when it seemed appropriate, they spoke about the rationale and the details of their faith; and some non-Christians, who noticed their modesty, their love for one another, and their care of the disadvantaged members of that society, asked them for the reason (1 Peter 3:15). Many, of course, did not ask. Sometimes especially thoughtful or bold or enthusiastic ones among the Christians—St. Paul, St. Stephen, or St. Peter—spoke openly; and again some of their hearers believed, though many did not. Moreover, as an often despised and suspect minority, believers in Christ expected suffering of one kind or another, including martyrdom. Their mentors had to warn them not to be "surprised at the fiery ordeal that comes upon you to prove you, as though something strange were happening" (1 Peter 4:12, RSV). The Acts of the Apostles amply testifies to this entire mode of being Christian, and we have domesticated and trivialized it by thinking it the mere beginnings of something that later on became what it was meant to become. To the contrary, it was and is the authentic way.

23. The Greek for fish is *ichthus,* and early Christians used each (Greek) letter of the word to fashion a statement about the core of their belief, thus: *Iesous Christos Theou Uios Soter* (Jesus Christ God's Son Savior). The graphic symbol of the fish (two simple curving lines convering to create the fish's tail) became a secret code by which Christians could identify one another.

In other language, if we take seriously the *sola scriptura* principle of the Reformation, the multicultural and religiously pluralistic context that we encounter in the book of Acts and in the Gospels and Epistles of the New Testament represents what is normal for Christians. It was normal in the early church; it has been normal in every new missional situation; it was normal in the Confessing Church in Germany's Nazi period and behind the iron curtain and in other places where Christianity was severely curtailed; and it is normal in most of the once reputedly Christian West today. In North America, many do not yet know that it is normal, or they repress the knowledge of it. Some even think, apparently, that what is normal for Christians is the sort of thing occurring as I write today in the bid of certain men for the leadership of the Republican Party in the USA, with each candidate trying to outdo the others with his true-believing Christianity. That, I would say, rather, is an anachronism, and it is already seen as such by more than half the population of the United States. It is already lampooned in the media. In fifty or a hundred years such Christian bravado will be the subject of ridicule in history books read by North American children.

No. Christendom, whether in its old-world pomposity or its new-world innocency and gaucheness, is effectively over. The relationship between Christianity and culture is being *normalized*. In place of the power-seeking and power-keeping church of the long Christendom centuries, we are returning to the biblical situation of the "little flock," which, *because* it is relatively little and *because* it does not see its destiny as becoming Big, is able in the midst of a highly diverse global situation to be "salt," "yeast," and "light"—concretely, to be a community of peacemaking, of justice seeking, and of stewardship of the good creation.

The key to living in such a pluralistic situation as a Christian or a Christian community is the assumption of a genuine modesty, a modesty born of *faith*, and, concomitantly, the relinquishment of all *religious* grasping and ambition. In such a modest community of faith, neither proselytism nor self-promotion nor theological triumphalism nor institutional imperialism has any place. The relation between Christ and culture can only be righted when the Christian community knows, and learns anew every day, that it is called to be very decidedly in this world, but that the source of its life, love, and hope is decidedly not of this world. That is the *basic* lesson Christians must learn and relearn.

The *second* stage in the task of separating Christian wheat from cultural chaff is entirely dependent, for its authenticity, on the acquisition of this first theological and attitudinal perspective. Once we are able to determine whether we are approaching this task as representative of the Christian religion or of faith in Jesus as the Christ, we may begin to deal with doctrinal and ethical specifics. That part of our task is enormous and will go on (I am tempted to say) world without end. Historical Christianity is like a huge snowball, now visibly melting in the sun of secularity and neopaganism. The original, small ball of snow, as it was pushed by willing hands through the centuries, grew very large indeed; but in addition to snow there had been rolled into it (some of it quite obviously so, some less conspicuously) layer after layer of extraneous matter. No doubt it is impossible at this stage fully to separate the snow from the great variety of stuff picked up along the way, but the attempt must be made, for much of what was rolled into the huge Christendom snowball is certainly not . . . Christianity!

It would be pretentious of me to suggest where such a monumental sorting-out would lead. Sensitive and insightful Christian scholars are working at the task today, and have been doing so for decades. It will and must continue. For our present purposes, and by way of concluding these reflections on Christianity and culture, I shall only propose a few questions of the sort which, in my opinion, serious Christians today and tomorrow ought to consider as they seek to distinguish the 'kernel' of faith—the *kerygma*—from its cultural accretions:

- Is Christianity as committed to capitalism as many in the capitalist-dominated Northern Hemisphere believe?

- What happened to the creation sagas of Genesis when the technological society of post-Enlightenment modernity got hold of the words "subdue" and "have dominion"? Is Christianity really so tied to 'Man' (*anthropos*) as many environmentalists have accused it of being?

- How have Victorian, bourgeois, and other forms of morality and sentiment colored the picture of Jesus most prevalent in contemporary American and Canadian Protestantism?

- What was lost when early Christians left behind Hebraic language and concepts and adapted their understanding of God, Jesus, humanity, and so forth to Greek, Hellenistic, and Latin languages and assumptions?

- Are church buildings really part of 'the plan'?

- Does the Bible insist that all clergy be paid salaries?

- What entered the Christian movement, a Jewish offshoot (grafted onto the Jewish tree, as Paul says), to enable it to become the spiritual background of Auschwitz?

- How did its affiliation with empire—from imperial Rome to imperial America—affect the church's self-understanding?

- Why did Easter, in the English-speaking world, become so prominent that Good Friday tended to be forgotten—especially by Protestants?

- The suffering of the church is the most conspicuous mark of the true church in the New Testament. Will the church of the future also suffer?

2

Not a Religion 'of the Book'

"The authority of the Bible was used to break
the proud authority of the church; whereupon
the Bible became another instrument
of human pride."[1]

PEOPLE OF THE BOOK?

NOTHING TANGIBLE IS MORE significant for Christians—and particularly for Protestant Christians—than are the Scriptures of the older and newer Testaments. Yet in this chapter I want to argue—and to do so quite consciously *as a Protestant*—that Christianity is not accurately described as a religion of the Book. The term *people of the Book* was used of Christians and Jews in the Qur'an (29:46), and it is sometimes employed by secular writers in describing Christians, Muslims, and Jews; but in this chapter I shall not be referring to these external sources. I have in mind rather the tendency within Christianity itself to identify itself by reference to the Bible in a special and often extremely misleading sense. I want to fault this identification for two basic reasons: first, associating this faith too exclusively with the Scriptures that Christians honor does an injustice to the breadth of Christianity; second, associating the Scriptures too exclusively with their function as religious authority (and "another instrument of human pride") does an injustice to the Scriptures themselves.

---

1. Reinhold Niebuhr, *The Nature and Destiny of Man* (New York: Scribner, 1953), 2: 231.

FUNDAMENTALISM AND BIBLICISM

This matter, like most, is especially conditioned today by ecclesiastical and religious circumstances and attitudes at work in our cultural context; therefore I will begin by presenting a thumbnail sketch of the relation of church and Bible in recent Protestant history, as I see it.

Particularly since the latter part of the nineteenth century a rather strange situation has developed in the Protestant conception of this relation—strange, I mean, from the vantage point of classical Protestantism. The sixteenth-century Reformers appealed to the Bible partly in order to challenge the authority of Rome. In the context of their struggle with the Catholic establishment, the Reformers sometimes made what today we may well regard as exaggerated claims for the Bible. Their approach to the Scriptures, however, should not be seen as being continuous with the biblical literalism characteristic of contemporary fundamentalism and other modern expressions of bibliocentrism. Fundamentalism, which made its first appearance in North America, can only be explained as a modern phenomenon. It could only come to be after the humanism of the Renaissance (which was still very much open to religion) had hardened into more independent and nontheistic forms of secularity, as happened in the eighteenth and nineteenth centuries. Over against this new tendency of human rationality to explain the world without reference to transcendence, conservative Christians, perhaps understandably enough, resorted to more and more dogmatic and authority-based expressions of the Christian faith. The Bible, which was certainly the epistemological engine of the Reformation, now became the chief bulwark against a post-Christian secular humanism that was experienced by conservative Christian groups as threatening to undo not only Christianity but the whole allegedly Christian civilization. This humanism, they felt, had infiltrated the churches themselves through liberal theological teachings and historical-critical approaches to the biblical writings. As in most situations of polarization, the conservative reaction to Christian liberalism and modernism was driven to increasingly bold claims for the biblical text. The verbal inerrancy of the Scriptures, one of the five fundamentals named by conservative groups meeting at Niagara in 1895, goes beyond anything that even the most Bible-centered Protestant thinkers of the Reformation period intended, as I shall try to show later. Fundamentalism represents, in fact, what from the perspective of classical Protestantism should be regarded as a quite new way of thinking about the Bible and the role of the Bible in Christian faith. Fundamentalists usually want to claim consistency with the Reformation, or some parts thereof; but serious scholars of history and biblical hermeneutics recognize this to be a spurious claim, born chiefly of the quest for authoritative roots. The biblicism that developed in North America and subsequently spread to other regions missionized by North American ultraconservatives is something quite new in the history of Christian thinking.

In Europe, the old flagship of Christendom, this new biblicism of America never gained a significant foothold. There, the older Reformation approaches to the Bible were never quite lost sight of, even though, in the seventeenth century and beyond, so-called Protestant Orthodoxy rather woodenized the livelier Reformation theology of the Bible, and later North American biblicists could recognize in this post-Reformation Orthodoxy some points of convergence. On our continent, however, and especially in the United States, literalistic interpretation of the Bible became—for a variety of reasons—more and more prominent; and in the twentieth century, at the level of popular religion, it achieved an extraordinary preeminence as a politically powerful force, which it retains to this day.

THE BIBLE IN THE NEW WORLD

Among the many reasons for this triumph of biblical literalism in North America, the following six could be noted:

1. Serious and disciplined biblical, theological, and historical reflection and scholarship that would have kept the more subtle traditions of the Reformation alive were never strong points of church life in North America. Piety, morality, and straightforward (often sloganized) dogma were more typical of New World Christianity than were theological scholarship or serious biblical exegesis.

2. Denominationalism—a growing multitude of churches and sects, each with its own favorite doctrinal and moral concerns and preferences—produced an atmosphere of ecclesiastical narrowness and certitude not hospitable to the kind of open inquiry that biblical study demands. In fact, fundamentalism is not so much interested in what the biblical text actually says as it is in finding in the biblical text proofs of its own *doctrinal* and *moral* presuppositions. An irony of Bible-thumping religion in North America is that the noisiest forms of it are frequently accompanied by abysmal ignorance about the Bible! As Bill McKibben writes in a splendid essay for *Harper's* magazine,

"Only 40 percent of Americans can name more than four of the Ten Commandments, and a scant half can cite any of the four Gospels. Twelve percent believe that Joan of Arc was Noah's wife."[2]

3. In their preaching, moderate and liberal Christians in our context increasingly turned away from biblical exposition and based their sermons on vaguely religious or popular themes, thus leaving the stewardship of the Scriptures to their more conservative interpreters.

4. The North American fascination with science and technology produced among religious conservatives, on the one hand, a fierce resistance against new scientific *theories* (particularly Darwinism) while, it encouraged, on the other hand, a kind of bid to "out-science" science in its quest for objective biblical truth.

5. The association of Christianity with Americanism, which we noted in the first chapter, required of the churches very straightforward, uncomplicated expressions of Christian teaching—expressions that could serve the political functions of a culture-religion. (When George W. Bush announced that "I don't do nuance"—perhaps his most honest pronouncement!—he was drawing upon a long and well-established tradition of American popular religion. The Bible itself, as centuries of painstaking biblical scholarship attests, is full of nuance, variety, paradox, and even apparent contradiction. But the public demand for straightforward and unambiguous assertion easily and regularly brushes over scriptural complexity).

6. Any enumeration of the reasons for the triumph of biblicism in North America would be incomplete, I think, if it did not notice the role of modern media. Commercially sponsored television in particular has facilitated the communication of the most simplistic, reductive, and (for many, alas) merely entertaining versions of the Christian religion that have ever been presented to such massive audiences. Though the image-based media may under certain conditions present theological, philosophical, and other complex subject matter in fresh and moving ways, in its role as mass communicator in the service of vested economic and other interests, television in particular seems custom made for the promulgation of the most conceptually crude ideas and messages.

2. McKibben, "The Christian Paradox: How a Faithful Nation Gets Jesus Wrong," *Harper's* (August 2005) 31–37.

For these and other reasons that could be adduced, Christianity in our present context, so far as the greater public of the United States and Canada is concerned, is practically identified with the kind of Bible religion, so called, that can be traced to this ultraconservative reaction to the advent of postreligious secularity—a reaction that some (e.g., Karen Armstrong)[3] say is the result of "embattled alienation" on the part of the fearful. So closely linked in the public mind is Christianity with this kind of biblicism that Christians who try to maintain a more nuanced approach to the Scriptures have a very difficult time doing so, even in university classrooms, and are often perceived both by other Christians and the nonchurched alike as having simply capitulated to the modern world. Even the more thoughtful among conservative Christian teachers often testify to this experience.

But the problem is still more complicated. For while conservative Christianity in North America has expressed itself in increasingly biblicistic terms, the more liberal churches of the old Protestant mainline seem to have left the playing field. They find it unproductive or distasteful to critique fundamentalism's approach to the Bible at the congregational level and to suggest an alternative way. The question of the nature and authority of Scripture has been left to the seminaries and scholars; and though the higher criticism of Scripture has been taught in theological colleges for well over a century, it has not filtered down into the pews. Most mainline Protestant laypersons today, I venture to say, are themselves so innocent of any informed awareness of the Reformation's theology of Scripture that they do not recognize any great discrepancy between classical Protestantism's approach to the Bible and what they hear about the Book from televangelists and their evangelical neighbors. Instead of trying to critique the biblicism of the most vociferous Christians on our continent, mainline Protestants, with few exceptions, appear to have resigned themselves to the captivation of the Scriptures by those who make the most noise about them. We clergy of the liberal and moderate mainline for the most part continue to preach to our congregations on themes and topics and issues rather than on textual interpretation, which is still by and large practiced in European Protestant settings. The actual study of the biblical text in our congregations is a rare and usually halfhearted pursuit or a springboard for personal opinion and experience sharing.

By default then, if not by design, the remnants of mainline Protestantism have quietly allowed the ownership of the Holy Scriptures to be

3. See Armsgtrong *The Battle for God* (New York: Knopf, 2000).

transferred, for all practical purposes, to Christian bodies whose approach to the Bible must be traced, not to the Reformation, but to a neurotic eighteenth- and nineteenth-century religious reaction against the cold winds of modernity.

Nothing is more needful today, I think, than that liberal and moderate Protestantism should seek to clarify and revive something of the essence of the classical Protestant approach to the Bible—modified, as it must be, by the discoveries and insights of biblical, theological, scientific, and other scholarship over the past century and a half. In what remains of this chapter, I want to suggest some of the points that such a revival of a genuinely Protestant approach to the Bible would necessarily entail:

THE BIBLE IN REFORMATION THOUGHT

(1) *The Bible and Sustained Study of the Bible Are Essential to Christian Life and Mission.*

There can be no doubt whatsoever that the Reformers taught that the Bible is indispensable to Christianity and the life of the Christian community. "Abandon scripture," warns Luther, "and God abandons us to the lies of men."[4] It was not only as a battering ram against the papacy that the Reformers turned to the Bible; far more important for them was the fact that the Bible put them in touch with gospel, good news to a languishing humanity. And it did so, not only in its New Testament Gospels and Epistles, however central these were as the testimony of the eyewitnesses to the Christ-event, but also in the older sacred writings of the Jews, *without which* (let me say at once) the newer Testament would have been for them unintelligible. In at least one place, Luther argued that *only* the Hebrew Scriptures (the Old Testament) should be called Holy Scripture, since that is how the New Testament itself refers to the older Testament. Certainly most of the Reformers interpreted the Hebrew Bible too allegorically for contemporary biblical scholarship, and one can find a disturbing supersessionism[5] in some of their ideas, but nothing in the writings of the major

---

4. E. Theodore Bachman, Introduction to Luther's essay, "A Brief Instruction on What to Look For and Expect in the Gospels," [1521], in *Word and Sacrament*, Part I, *Luther's Works* (Philadelphia: Muhlenberg, 1960), 116.

5. That is, the belief that revealed truth as manifested in Jesus Christ and the biblical testimony to his life, death, and resurrection, *supersedes* the religion of the Jews, including the Old Testament, when it is not illumined by Christian interpretation.

Reformers that could be called marcionitic,[6] nothing shows a readiness to dispense with the Old Testament. Rather, in their writing and preaching they range over the whole Bible and make the public reading and private study of all of it (excepting the Apocrypha) mandatory to Christian life and calling.

However, they never present the Bible as if *it* were the object or principal focus of faith.

(2) *The Bible is understood as means, not as end.*

The Reformation produced several famous slogans starting with or including the Latin word signifying exclusivity: *solus* or *sola*, meaning "only" or "solely"—*sola gratia* (grace alone), *sola fide* (faith alone), *sola scriptura* (Scripture alone), and (perhaps the most important of all) *per Christum solum* (through Christ alone). And to these we should add *soli Deo gloria*, John Calvin's particular motto: "glory to God *alone*." Reformation scholarship, however, makes a distinction between *sola gratia*, *sola fide*, and *per Christum solum* on the one hand, and *sola scriptura* on the other. The first group (by grace alone, by faith alone, through Christ alone) treats of the *substance* or content of the faith, and consequently is commonly referred to as signifying the *material* principle of the Reformation. By contrast, *sola scriptura* (by Scripture alone) is designated the *formal* principle of the Reformation. In other words, grace, faith, God, and the belief in Jesus as the Christ represent the subject matter or substance of our faith—the *what* of belief; the Scriptures represent the form in which this substance comes to us: the *how* of its communication. Classical Protestantism does not ask us to believe in the Bible (an expression one can frequently hear from evangelicals and others). The Bible *itself* does not ask us to believe in it! It asks us to believe in God, made especially manifest to us in Jesus as the Christ, through the testimony of the Holy Spirit. Believing in the Bible as such is just as much idolatry as is believing in the church or in this or that codification of Christian doctrinal tradition. The term *bibliolatry*, meaning excessive veneration of the Bible, came to be used in late nineteenth- and twentieth-century religious discourse in response to this idolatry of Bible worship. As Reinhold Niebuhr ironically wrote, "The authority of the Bible was used to break the proud authority of the church: whereupon the Bible became another instrument of human pride."[7]

6. Marcion, who died in 160 CE, rejected entirely the Old Testament.

7. Niebuhr, *The Nature and Destiny of Man* (New York: Scribner, 1953), 2:231.

The Bible itself spurns such bibliocentrism. There is in fact a consistent and essential modesty about itself in this amazing collection of writings that we call the Bible. Only a few isolated verses may be found to back any more pretentious view. Classical Protestantism affirms that Christian belief is mediated in significant measure *through* the Bible, but it stops far short of making the Bible the object and end of faith. That is why, thirdly—

3) The term "Word of God" should not be <u>unqualifiedly</u> applied to the Bible.

The term *Word of God* is certainly and rightly attributed to Protestant usage. Generation after generation, congregations have been urged to "hear the Word of God" when they were read to from the Bible in church services. This usage, however, can be—and I think has been—subtly misleading; for it too unqualifiedly equates God's Word with the written word.

Karl Barth performed an immense service for Protestants (of which alas all too few Protestants have availed themselves!) when he distinguished what he called "the threefold form" of the divine Word: the word preached, the word written, and the Word incarnate.[8] Only the last-mentioned form, the Word made flesh, he insisted, can the church regard unqualifiedly as the Word of God. The written word bears witness to that living Word, and preaching, when it is faithful, lends to the scriptural words an indispensable dimension of contemporaneity, bringing them to life for us. But these two forms of the divine word can only point, and point rather awkwardly, to the incarnate word.

This is what the prologue of the Gospel of John declares too, explicitly about the incarnation of the Word and implicitly about the other two forms. "In the beginning was the Word . . . and the Word became flesh and lived among us" (John 1:1–14, NRSV). Here the Bible itself rejects all reductive versions of divine Truth, including the reduction of God's Word to the words of Scripture. God's Truth is a living truth. *Jesus did not deliver truths; he lived Truth among us.*[9]

In fact, when he wanted to be quite definitive, Barth would not say that the Bible *is* the Word of God, but only that it *becomes* God's Word if and when its words are taken up by the divine Spirit and made to address us. What then can we say of this book in itself?, Barth asks. His answer is subtle but extremely perceptive:

8. Barth, *Church Dogmatics* 1/1, 1–310.

9. See chapter 5, below.

Of the book as we have it, we can only say: We recollect that we have heard in this book the Word of God; we recollect, in and with the Church, that the Word of God has been heard in all this book, and in all parts of it; therefore we expect that we shall hear the Word of God in this book again, and hear it even in those places where we ourselves have not heard it before. Yet the presence of the Word of God itself, the real and present speaking and hearing of it, is not identical with the existence of the book as such. But in this presence something takes place in and with the book, for which the book as such does indeed give the possibility, but the reality of which cannot be anticipated or replaced by the existence of the book. A free decision is made. It then comes about that the Bible, the Bible *in concreto*, this or that biblical context, i.e. the Bible as it comes to us in this or that specific measure is taken and used as an instrument in the hand of God, i.e. it speaks to and is heard by us as the authentic witness to divine revelation and is therefore present as the Word of God.[10]

No modern exposition of Christianity has been more thoroughly informed by the Bible than has the theology of Karl Barth; but in the quotation I have just cited one has an explicit (if highly nuanced) statement of why it is misleading to think of Christianity as a religion of the Book. The Book—or rather, this remarkable *collection* of writings representative of a thousand years of reflection on the things of God[11]—should certainly be

10. Barth, *Church Dogmatics* 1/2, ed. G. W. Bromiley and T. F. Torrance (Edinburgh: T. and T. Clark, 1956), 530.

11. The word *Bible* is derived directly from the Greek word for "book" (*biblos*), and this, plus the fact that (normally) we have this amazing collection of writings in one book, between two covers, has fostered among Christians and others the notion that the Holy Scriptures of Christianity consist precisely of *one book*. That is of course far from the case. What Christians have, as Holy Writ, is in fact an extremely diverse collection of very different kinds of writings: historical or prehistorical accounts; law and commentary on divine law; devotional material like the Psalms; spiritual meditations and wisdom literature; reminiscences on the life and teachings of Jesus; letters of prominent early Christian leaders (Paul especially) to the small, evolving churches of the first century; apocalyptic literature; and so forth.

This plurality of writings sacred to Israel and the Christian movement is not incidental to its meaning for faith. As books (not *a book*) the very form of our Holy Scriptures warns against strict uniformity of doctrine and practice—or, otherwise stated, it does not lend itself to an *ideological* approach to faith. "Beware the man of one book" is a statement attributed to St. Thomas Aquinas; and scholars are divided as to the meaning of this *bon mot*. But one dominant tradition insists that Thomas meant that we should not be ready, as believers, to give ourselves wholeheartedly to one point of view, but should listen to many, reflect on all, and come to our own conclusions. If that was Thomas's meaning,

revered; but it should never be worshiped or treated as something suprahu-man. It is not, but only becomes God's Word for us when the mystery of the Spirit causes it to be so.

Now an interesting consequence of this Barthian teaching about the Word of God (and I think it is strictly consistent with Reformation thought on the subject) is that when the Word of God is identified unqualifiedly with the person of Jesus Christ, it prevents any sort of pretention to our own Christian ownership of truth. For while churches and individuals may possess Bibles, they certainly cannot possess the Person called the Christ—who in the same Gospel of John dares to say to his disciples, "I *am* the Truth"[12]—which is not the height of egotism, if it is understood in context, but the most radical statement of truth's livingness and nonpossessibility.

I have never forgotten an incident that happened about fifty years ago and that clarified this teaching for me in an unforgettable way. During my second or third year at Union Theological Seminary in New York City, the committee in charge of worship determined to invite to James Chapel the most popular, new, and youngish evangelical preacher of the day: Billy Graham. Billy has become very respectable in his old age (as some of us appear to do), but at that time he was "full of beans," and obviously terribly conscious of being in the lions' den, the hotbed of theological liberalism on this continent. I remember how, at one point in his conspicuously defensive sermon, he held up his copy of the Scriptures and shouted, "I've got it right here in the Bible." And, neophyte though I was then, I knew exactly what were, for Billy, hiddenly, the most important words in that sentence. They were the first three words, "*I've got it*"; the implication, in that context, was, "and you don't, you benighted liberals!" And I thought to myself, But Billy, *it* isn't to be *got*, this truth you're daring to claim you have. It's not to be had, bandied about, held aloft, used as a battering ram against others, in short, possessed! God's truth wants to have you, but you can never have it, my dear Billy. You can only listen for it, and try to let it illumine your path day by day.

Of course, when ministers or lectors bid us, in divine service, to "Hear the Word of God" in the biblical passage they are about to read, what they really mean, if they are knowledgeable about it, is, "I hope you will hear in

---

it applies very appropriately to the Bible, for it is by no means one book, even though its many authors are united in their concentration on one center—the divine/human relationship.

12. See chapter 5, below.

this passage I am about to read something so ultimately meaningful to you that you will regard it as God's own word to you." However, human nature being what it is, and spiritual hubris being what it is, this kind of careful distinction is rarely perceived in the formula. Perhaps we should be truer to the aforementioned modesty of this Book and simply say, "Hear the written witness to God's Word." But of course we really do hope that the reading of Scripture in the congregation will stir the minds and hearts of the hearers so deeply that they will in fact "*hear the Word of God*" and not just words, words, words.

This leads to my fourth thesis about classical Protestantism's teaching on the Bible, and it is this:

> *(4) The biblical testimony to the Word of God is inspired. But this inspired testimony cannot by itself inspire us. The outward testimony of the written Word requires another, inward testimony—which tradition designated the <u>testimonium Spiritus Sancti internum</u>, the internal testimony of the Holy Spirit.*

To elaborate a little on this thesis, I am going to take the bull by the horns and turn to John Calvin. Poor Calvin is more frequently than any other Reformer made the author of biblical literalism. This only demonstrates how very far the truncation of Protestantism has gone. Calvin certainly believed that the Bible was "inspired," and indeed that it was inspired in the fullness of its testimony. He taught that in this written witness to the triune God and God's dealings with creation, God "opens his own sacred mouth"; "[He] not only proclaims that some god ought to be worshipped, but at the same time pronounces that he himself is the Being to whom worship is due." If we really hear, truly hear, hearingly hear, the Bible's witness, Calvin believed, we shall know that we are being addressed by the God's own voice. The biblical message has communicated itself to us when we are caused to hear its words "as if [we] heard [these] very words pronounced by God himself." Note well: "as if"! Calvin does not say of these biblical words that they *are* God's very words, frozen forever in indelible written form. He is a much more sophisticated theologian than that! For him, human words, however luminous and inspired, could no more contain and communicate *God's* Word than could human-made bread and wine contain Christ's body and blood. (I refer to his teaching on the Eucharist, which much more than Luther's denied the Catholic concept of transubstantiation.)[13] As with the

13. Calvin's view of the sacrament is often termed *consubstantiation*, meaning that

bread and wine, the words, if they are to be heard hearingly, profoundly, have to be caught up and transformed by a testimony far more mysterious than language, which itself is eminently mysterious—the testimony of the Holy Spirit: "the testimony of the Spirit," he writes, "is superior to all reason. For as God alone is a sufficient witness of himself in his own word, so also the word will never gain credit in the hearts of men, until it be confirmed by the internal testimony of the Spirit."

Yes, Calvin believed in the literal (or one might better say), the full literary inspiration of the Bible. He was educated, after all, in the humanist tradition, whose cry was *Ad fontes*—"back to the sources!" But he certainly would not accept—I suspect he would not even comprehend!—the kind of dogged, literalistic approach that finds every word of the Bible (but in which versions and translations?) uttered by God personally and directly. The truth is, surely, that between Calvin and modern biblicism a great historical-hermeneutical gulf is fixed, and the only possible steppingstone from the former to the latter is that Protestant Orthodoxy of the seventeenth century and beyond, which exchanged the plenary inspiration of Scripture taught by Calvin for a prosaic and fundamentally unspiritual literalism. As the Reformed theologian the late Hendrikus Berkhof writes, while Calvin taught the literal inspiration of the Bible, he left this in quite general terms; but "the inspiration doctrine of [later] Protestant Scholasticism . . . eventually left no room for the individual authors of the Bible other than that of being stenographers of the dictation of the Spirit."[14] For Calvin, the inspiration of the divine Spirit was not only required back then (required by the authors of these texts), it is required now for us to receive them as sacred and to begin to understand what their message is. It would be more accurate, accordingly, to say that for Calvin Christianity is a religion of the Spirit rather than to say that it is a religion of the Book; but he would not want us to indulge ourselves in either characterization, and like Luther would insist that Spirit and Word belong together.[15]

Christ is present *with* the congregation as they participate in the Lord's Supper.

14. Hendrikus Berkhof, *Christian Faith: An Introduction to the Study of the Faith*, trans. Sierd Woudstra (Grand Rapids: Eerdmans, 1979), 88.

15. The references to Calvin are all from book 1, chapters 6 and 7, and the translation is that of John Allen, as published in *Institutes of the Christian Religion* (Philadelphia: Presbyterian Board of Education, 1936), 1:85ff.

> *(5) There are choices to be made, always, between the more and*
> *the less authoritative portions of Scripture, and the Reformers—*
> *Luther especially—did not hesitate to do so.*

It is a very interesting thing that those Christians today and yesterday who make so much of a point about the inspiration of every word of Scripture in fact pay these respects chiefly to the doctrinal and moral teachings of the Bible with which they feel particularly at home, or that they can make to seem proof-texts for their salient religious, ethical, and political concerns. A notorious example of this is found in that brand of Christian conservativism that arranged itself in the train of Adolf Hitler: it made much of chapter 13 of Paul's letter to the Romans, which counsels obedience to the "governing authorities," but it famously overlooked the antiracist teachings of the two Testaments such as that same Paul the Apostle's insistence that in Christ there is "no longer Jew or Greek, there is no longer slave or free, there is no longer male and female" (Galatians 3:28, NRSV). Similarly, it is noteworthy that the Christians in North America today who pour over and magnify the Bible's seven pretty obscure references to homosexuality have little or nothing to say about the biblical laws against usury (the collection of interest) and other expressions of inordinate acquisitiveness, to say nothing of its positive teaching concerning the priority of love over every form of personal purity and self-righteousness.

Choices have always to be made concerning the weight that is to be given to explicit biblical texts. This is not a discovery of the Jesus Seminar! Luther, whose theology of biblical authority is, I think, the least known, in Anglo-Saxon denominations, of any of the Reformers, did not hesitate to leap into the fray at this point. He certainly believed, in Calvin's general sense of the term, in the overall inspiration of the Scriptures. Noteworthy is one important writing, caustically titled, *Answer to the Hyperchristian, hyperspritual, and hyper-learned Book by Goat Emser in Leipzig—including some thoughts regarding his companion, the fool Murner.* (They didn't go in for snappy titles in those halcyon days, and they didn't care a bit about political correctness—Emser and Murner were both Catholics.) In this particular writing Luther insists that the actual text of the Scriptures have to be strictly adhered to, for he sees the funny combination of Roman doctrinal objectivism and pietistic subjectivity as a great danger. *Listen to the text*, he demands, and don't assume that you already know on the basis of your doctrine and your fine spiritual nature what it is going to say! Over against both conservative dogmatism and liberal personalism this is still pretty good advice!

But Luther was not about to become a textual literalist in the contemporary sense. Though his knowledge of the biblical texts is astounding by any standards of judgment, he was never tempted to lend the text the distinction of ultimate truth. I think this is because he knew the biblical texts so very well. Not only was his work at Wittenberg the work of a *biblical* as distinct from a *systematic* or dogmatic theologian, but he spent the whole of his life revising his original translations of the older and newer Testaments. He was at pains, always, to find just the right words; and for him the right words were not only German words that could reproduce accurately, or at least adequately, the original Greek and Hebrew texts, but words that the common people, his German contemporaries, could comprehend. When he labored in the Wartburg fortress on his original translation of the New Testament, he would call stable boys and others to his aid: "How would you describe this experience, or put that thought into words?" Though he was not a great linguist in the manner of Erasmus or Zwingli and other learned humanists, Luther had a profound feeling for the same kind of thing that caused the writers of the New Testament to compose their accounts in Koine, or common, Greek rather than in classical Greek—namely, so that the people for whom these Scriptures are intended should be able, potentially, to hear them with some beginnings of comprehension. Oh, Luther knew the Bible—and yet . . .

With what still amazes biblical conservatives, if they know about it, he dismissed or took lightly whole sections of it, including (famously) the Epistle of James and the Apocalypse. He had theological or apologetic reasons for doing so, and he acknowledged these. But behind this seemingly cavalier approach to scriptural authority was Luther's intelligent awareness of the great *variety* of biblical teachings, and his honesty in recognizing that, without confusion and contradiction, the whole of this diverse and immensely rich deposit of Judeo-Christian spirituality could not be regarded as equally binding. He recognized that some principle or principles of hermeneutics (or interpretation) would have to be decided upon; and the principle that commended itself to him most insistently was expressed by him in the German phrase *was Christum treibet* ("what drives to Christ"). That is, in general the authority of Scripture and of its various parts and claims is to be seen in the intensity of its witness to the Christ. Luther did not understand this in a narrow or dogmatic sense. For him, after all,

Christ was not to be equated with any dogmatically explicit Christology; the Christ, the Messiah, was disclosed to faith in the person, Jesus, and this person, not only on account of his divinity (so called) but in his ordinary humanity too infinitely transcends our ideas about this person.

Now this very christocentric approach to Scripture could, and on occasion did, lead Luther into some assumptions that, today, we would want to criticize rather severely. Particularly, it colored his Old Testament exegesis by reading the New into the Old by means of allegory and so on; and accordingly it also aided and abetted, alas, his unfortunate and rather absurd and uninformed attitude towards Jews—both of these things, unfortunately, prejudices that he shared with most medieval and later Christianity. Nevertheless, the principle *what drives to Christ*, provided Luther with a unifying comprehension of the intention of biblical faith, and it did so in a manner much less offensive than other hermeneutic principles that have been employed in the service of biblical interpretation; for, as I have already maintained, unlike most interpretational principles, this christocentrism, when it is profoundly grasped, has a built in impediment to absolutism: Jesus Christ is Thou, and as he is testified to by both the Word and the Spirit, he resists every attempt to reduce him to an It.

(6) Listening to the Bible always involves listening to the Zeitgeist.

Karl Barth's well-known statement that doing theology means having the Bible in one hand and the newspaper in the other is a genuine representation of Reformation thought—particularly, though by no means exclusively, that of Luther. There can be no genuine discernment of biblical witness that is not simultaneously a struggle to discern the spirit of the times (cf. Luke 12:56). As Gerhard Ebeling has written, "This striving for a true understanding of the scripture, with its concern for the Spirit, is of necessity concerned with the present existential situation."[16]

That situation is never still and unchanging. Change is in fact the name of the game—of the game of life as well as the game of human attempts to understand life. The quest for gospel, therefore, always entails an often excruciating endeavor on the part of the disciple community to intuit the real character of the time and place in which it finds itself. Not every word or emphasis of the Bible is appropriate everywhere. Prophetic faith

---

16. Gerhard Ebeling, *Luther: An Introduction to His Thought,* trans. R. W. Wilson (Philadelphia: Fortress, 1977), 99–100.

always looks for the right word, the *appropriate* word, the "word from the Lord." Gospel is not a fixed message; it is a message that the church itself always has to discover anew, for its aim is to engage, address, and change the actual human situation. Reformation theology of the Scriptures is at base (without using the term, of course) *contextual* theology. And no one statement of this contextuality is more moving, still today, than Luther's distinction between the profession and the confession of Christ—which I have made, almost, the motto of my own attempts at theological work:

> If I profess with the loudest voice and clearest exposition every portion of the truth of God except precisely that little point which the world and the devil are at that moment attacking, I am not *confessing* Christ, however boldly I may be *professing* him. Where the battle rages, there the loyalty of the soldier is proved, and to be steady on all the battlefield besides is mere flight and disgrace if he flinches at that point.[17]

CONCLUSION: THE BIBLE AND THE CHRISTIAN FUTURE

With this I shall conclude: There is only one absolute authority for Reformation thought—the authority of the One who transcends all the authorities: the authority of the Voice the prophets believed they heard out of a burning bush, from a mountaintop, in dreams and night callings, in the midst of a suffering and exiled people; the authority the apostles experienced in the call of an itinerant and unrecognized rabbi to discipleship. Of all the provisional authorities honored by the Christian movement in its long history (tradition, the councils and creeds of Christian beginnings, the reasonable musings of those who tried to understand what they believed, the spiritual experiences of saints and mystics, the ministry and mind of the church here and now), the Bible, for Protestants, is by far the most significant. But it too is . . . provisional—and in both senses of that term, namely, it is provided by a provident God, and it is given for the time being, pending (as it were) more permanent arrangements! Christianity cannot, therefore, be rightly

---

17. Quoted from *Luther's Works* (Weimar edition) Letters 3:81ff. in Hall, "The Diversity of Christian Witnessing in the Tension between Subjection to the Word and Relation to the Context," in *Luther's Ecumenical Significance*, ed. Peter Manns and Harding Meyer (Philadelphia: Fortress, 1984), 257.

and adequately characterized as a religion of the Book, so far as classical Protestantism is concerned, despite 'the book's' indispensability.

The future of Protestantism, I think, must lie in a recovery of this complex but by no means undecipherable classical Protestant understanding of the place of the Bible in Christian life and mission. Where will such a recovery be possible? In recent years, I have often had to conclude that the genesis of such a recovery might well occur in a manner surprising to many liberal Christians. For I have noticed how frequently it happens that students of theology with backgrounds in evangelical and even fundamentalist communities of faith, especially by the time they reach graduate studies, have proven to be the most engaged and astute theologians. The reason for this, I think, is not hard to grasp. However narrowly they may have been conditioned by biblicism, they at least have familiarity with the biblical text, while those coming to the study of theology out of liberal and moderate ecclesiastical backgrounds are often innocent of—and sometimes condescending towards—biblical knowledge. Given at least the beginnings of knowledge about the Bible, however restricted it may be, conservative Christians who learn through actual experience of critical scriptural exegesis that it is not the demonic thing they were taught to assume, and who through their growing experience of the multilayered problematic of life in the contemporary world learn to hear the Bible with the ears of contemporaries—such Christians, in my experience at least, often turn out to be the most informed and contextually engaged theologians of all.

This, so far as it is true, suggests one pressing message for the remnants of so-called mainline Protestantism today: Get to know your Bible! Don't allow your distaste for biblicism to turn you away from study of the Bible. Don't imagine that because you have discovered a great many pressing social issues, or your own rare spirituality, or the marvels of the Internet, that you can keep this book, unconsulted, on some ornamental shelf or end table! Truly, the Christian faith is not a religion of the Book; but without the Book this faith can have, I suspect, no significant future.

3

Not Doctrine

The Moment I take Christianity as a doctrine and so indulge
my cleverness and profundity or my eloquence or my
imaginative powers in depicting it, people are very pleased;
I am looked upon as a serious Christian.
The Moment I begin to express existentially what I say,
and consequently to bring Christianity into reality,
it is as though I had exploded existence—the scandal is
there at once.[1]

CHRISTIAN DOCTRINE:
NECESSARY AND COMPICATED

THE WORD DOCTRINE COMES directly from the Latin *doctrina*, which
means the teaching or body of teachings associated with a belief system.
Like all religions, and indeed every system of belief whether religious or
secular, Christianity involves a body of doctrine. Christianity is in fact rich
in doctrine; many would say overly so! Compared with Islam, which Sir
Kenneth Clark claimed is the simplest religious creed ever to have gained
acceptance,[2] the Christian religion abounds in theological variety, com-

---

1. Søren Kierkegaard, quoted by the Rev. Harold Alston, Fort Nelson, BC, October
1977; source unknown.

2. "The strength of Islam was its simplicity. The early Christian Church had dissipated its strength by theological controversies, carried on for three centuries with incred-
ible violence and ingenuity. But Mahomet, the prophet of Islam, preached the simplest
doctrine that has ever gained acceptance; and it gave to his followers the invincible solidarity that had once directed the Roman legions. In a miraculously short time—about

plexity, and nuance—to the point that it is practically impossible for most Christians to follow the complicated turnings and shadings of professional theological reflection. It requires years of concentrated study to acquire a sophisticated grasp of, for example, the evolution of the doctrine of the Trinity or of the Person of Jesus, the Christ. There are reasons for this, and we shall consider them presently; but first we must honestly acknowledge this complexity and its affects upon the life and composition of the church.

Perhaps the most problematic consequence of the doctrinal complexity of Christianity is that it tends to resolve itself into two levels of Christian belonging: a small, highly educated elite, and a large body of persons who may to a certain extent have been indoctrinated but far too often are merely passive believers in what they have been told is required of Christians by way of personal assent.[3] Throughout most of the history of Christianity, but in particular after this religion's fourth-century establishment as the dominant religion of the West, this division between the knowledgeable few and the submissive majority has been both typical and a source of contention. During the High Middle Ages, when theological discourse became increasingly rarefied, brilliant, and (often enough) aggressive, the masses of Christians, including even aristocratic elements of society, were incapable of following the discussion of the schools, and were not even expected to do so. Priests and preachers condensed doctrine into simple tenets and moral precepts that were often mixed with purely ecclesiastical concern; laity were expected to believe on the authority of those who had the leisure, learning, and discipline to study these complexities.

The Renaissance and, in particular, the Reformation altered this situation significantly through the introduction of preaching and teaching that consciously made the attempt to *explain* Scripture and doctrine, catechetical classes and lay instruction, direct access to the Bible in the common tongue, and, withal, through the promulgation of the radical idea that ordinary people were capable of understanding much more than they had been given credit for. The Enlightenment of the eighteenth century, resulting in a decisive dampening of ecclesiastical authority and the introduction of public education, encouraged in the churches (notably in Protestant churches

---

fifty years—the classical world was overrun. Only its bleached bones stood out against the Mediterranean sky." Clark, *Civilization: A Personal View* (Harmondsworth, UK: Penguin, 1982), 22.

3. Even most clergy, whose formal theological studies normally require only three of four years, would be had pressed to articulate the major stages in the development of Trinitarian doctrine or to explain the Formula of Chalcedon.

of northern Europe and the New World) the inauguration of confirmation classes, Sunday schools, and other forms of Christian education (e.g., adult Bible study).

Despite this opening up of doctrinal examination and free discussion, however, the feeling has lingered among many lay Christians that Christianity entails adherence to certain doctrines—doctrines which, for the most part, defy satisfactory explanation or at least transcend ordinary rationality, and that must therefore simply be accepted as revealed truth. Those who cannot accept these doctrines, or who entertain a persistent skepticism about their verity, either are pushed toward the edges of their community of belief or in some instances work actively to change the ethos of their community. The latter tendency has been greatly accelerated in recent centuries. Today's liberal and moderate Christian denominations are the consequences of what might be called a quiet rebellion against established doctrine. In fact, it would not be altogether incorrect to say that Christianity today, particularly but not exclusively Protestant Christianity, consists of a spectrum whose character is partly determined by varying attitudes toward doctrine. Some communities see doctrine as definitive and mandatory, some hold doctrinal norms lightly, and for yet others doctrine is uninteresting.

In keeping with the basic approach of this study, I shall argue that Christianity is not and must not be reduced to doctrine. Yet, contrary to liberal laissez faire, I do not believe that doctrine is either dispensable or optional. It is present even in allegedly noncreedal communities of Christian belief.[4] In what follows, we shall consider: (1) the reasons why *Christian* doctrine is necessarily complex, (2) the quite different attitudes and practices to which this complexity leads, and (3) the evolving role of doctrine in the post-Christendom situation.

WHY IS CHRISTIAN DOCTRINE SO COMPLEX?

Let us first dispense with the childish idea that Christian doctrine is complex simply because ecclesiastical authorities and professional theologians

---

4. "[T]he 'creedless Christianity' professed by a number of groups (including, for example, many Quakers and the Disciples of Christ) is not genuinely creedless. When creedlessness is insisted on as a mark of group identity, it becomes by definition operationally creedal." George A Lindbeck, *The Nature of Doctrine: Religion and Theology in a Postliberal Age* (Philadelphia: Westminster, 1984), 74.

make it so. To be sure, neither the propensity of religious authority to impose belief on others, nor the proclivity of theologians to indulge in unnecessarily convoluted rhetoric, nor even obscurantism, is to be discounted; yet there are *inherent* reasons why Christian teaching is necessary, and why it cannot be as simple as many want it to be.[5] We should consider these before we introduce more critical thoughts concerning the use and abuse of doctrine.

1) *The Profound Complexity of the Simple Gospel.* The narrative concerning the events centered in Jesus of Nazareth, which constituted the basis for what the earliest Christians proclaimed as gospel, is itself not as simple and straightforward as it is perennially made out to be by pious believers and enthusiastic evangelists. To speak only of the Gospels, we note that there are *four* of them—that is to say four significantly distinctive accounts which share important themes, but that despite well-known efforts to do so, cannot be easily harmonized into a single story or point of view. Moreover, these Gospels cannot simply stand on their own but require interpretation. The need for exegesis and interpretation of the core events of Christian beginnings is demonstrated concretely by the fact that St. Paul had already begun that hermeneutical or theological process before the Synoptic Gospels (Matthew, Mark, and Luke) had appeared or had achieved a wide hearing. The belief, popular in liberal circles, that Paul *complicated* the simple gospel with his theological agenda and its intricacies is itself simplistic in the extreme. Paul was doing what had to be done if the Christian message were to avoid being confined to occurrences in a small country at the eastern end of the Mediterranean Sea: namely, he situated these events in the history and promise of an ancient people, Israel, and, to the best of his ability, described their universal—even their cosmic—significance. Paul achieved this remarkable and courageous intellectual feat not only without *contradicting* the oral and later written tradition, but by drawing upon and expanding its depth and significance. Had we been left with the gospel accounts only, we should either have had to do the kind of thing that Paul did, or else the story of the Christ would have remained a brief episode in the long story of the struggles of the Jewish people. To be sure, Paul's illuminations of the meaning of the events centered in Jesus themselves introduce further complications, as any attempt at interpreting what are believed to be revelatory events is destined to do.

5. See the discussion of this in relation to Andrew Sullivan in the Conclusion, p. 158.

2) *The Bible's Unresolved Problems.* A second reason why Christian doctrine is inherently complex is that the New Testament itself, Gospels and Epistles together, begged many questions that the early church could not ignore. Chief among these problems, of course, was the relation of Jesus Christ to the God of Abraham, Isaac, and Jacob—the One God of Hebraic monotheism. It is true that both the doctrine of the Trinity and the concept of Christ's two natures (divine and human) are not *biblical* doctrines, and that, therefore, those who wish doctrine to be strictly subordinate to Scripture[6] have often had difficulty with these terms. But that they—or something like them—were made necessary by the testimony of the Scriptures, conceived as a unity of Old and New Testaments, is obvious enough. Clearly, the Christians were not prepared to confess that Jesus of Nazareth was merely a wise teacher or a prophet or one among many representatives of the Deity. They experienced Jesus as the Christ, the promised Messiah, the very Word of God present and incarnate in their midst. But how could they do this while holding strictly to the faith of Israel? They were not about to forfeit that foundational theology and wander into the dangerous territory of polytheism. They were after all (for the most part) Jews!

Serious Christians have long acknowledged, therefore, that the doctrines both of the incarnation and of the Trinity *evolved.* Most also acknowledge that it is extremely complicated to follow the agonizing and divisive discussions, struggles, and councils that led to creedal statements more or less acceptable to the majority. Both historically and theologically, the doctrines of the Trinity and of the person of the Christ are complex; but those who would avoid this complexity in favor of something more immediately accessible to human thought and experience must answer the question why, in any case, Jesus should be at the center of this faith—ergo why Christianity should exist at all! Christianity is by definition christocentric. This does not mean that Christianity is centerd in the Christ *exclusively* (i.e., it is not christomonistic)—that would be a contradiction of the very character and mission of the Christ, biblically viewed. But it does mean that Christianity is what it is because the figure at the center of its life and its message is more mysterious, unique and of ultimate significance to faith

---

6. Calvin, for instance, "could wish that the terms 'Trinity' and 'person' were buried, provided that those who objected to them—as absent from Scripture and 'fashioned by the human mind'—agreed on 'the faith that Father, Son, and Spirit are one God, yet the Son is not the Father, nor the Spirit the Son, but that they are differentiated by their particular characteristics." Hans J. Hillerbrand, *The Encyclopaedia of Protestantism* (New York: Routledge, 2004), 2:607.

than a merely human figure could be. It is indeed probable that Christianity would not have emerged into history as a distinctive faith had not the early church, pushed by the biblical record, insisted that this "despised and rejected" human being was, *in reality,* far more than a prophet or a failed Messiah. It is also probable that Christianity would effectively cease to be were its adherents no longer prepared to see anything in Jesus beyond that which could be explained in purely human and rational terms. Those today who want to keep Jesus at the center but without any theological complications are depending on the residue of the faith of earlier generations of Christians, who risked theological complication in order to keep Jesus at the center.

3. Christian Mission—the Need to Communicate. A third reason for the complexity of Christian doctrine stems from the inherent necessity of this faith to address itself to particular, changing circumstances and cultures. The main stream of Christianity was never content, as were the mystery religions, to remain a discreet and secret society. The good news had to be proclaimed, shared, communicated!

But such communication requires great sensitivity to the ethos of those to whom the gospel is addressed. Contexts affect the telling of the story.[7] Even before the end of the first century CE, Christianity found itself in the midst of a world that spoke a language quite different from the language of Jesus and his first followers. The dominant language of that world—its *lingua franca*—was Greek. Paul could engage in his ecumenical mission because he knew Greek. But he was a Jew. How could one translate into Greek a narrative and message formulated in the quite different linguistic, religious, and cultural context of Judaism? After years of painstaking biblical and linguistic studies, we know today that the movement of Christianity from Jerusalem to Athens (to speak figuratively) introduced into Christian discourse a whole new set of problems: for language is never just language; it is the bearer of a worldview, and much is (as one says) lost in translation. One may ask, for instance, whether the language of the Nicene Creed and the Chalcedonian christological formula accurately conveyed the earliest church's understanding of God and Jesus as the Christ. Certainly Peter and the others would not have understood the language or Nicaea, but would they have understood the ideas? That, I would say, is very doubtful.

7. See Douglas John Hall, *Thinking the Faith: Christian Theology in a North American Context* (Minneapolis: Augsburg, 1989), 69–246.

This earliest move of Christianity to a foreign context was of course followed by countless subsequent encounters with new languages and cultures; for the missiological thrust of Christian faith meant that Christians, unlike Jews, were not content simply to live among other peoples, but were impelled by their faith to translate their message into the conceptual and linguistic worlds of all those among whom they moved. Thus a considerable part of the complexity of Christian doctrine stems from the contextualizing necessity of this faith tradition. And this necessity involves not only a spatial but a temporal dimension: what is gospel in one historical milieu is not necessarily or appropriately gospel in another historical moment. To comprehend Christian doctrine, therefore, one must achieve not only a rather sophisticated theological acumen but also a sensitivity to history and change.

4. *Human Complexity, Resistance, and Doubt.* The gospel may be simple, but *we* are not! Surely a major component of the complexity of Christian doctrine must be traced precisely to this—that is, to the labyrinth of our human spirits and minds. To begin with, every one of the major doctrines of Christianity requires a serious and sustained effort of intellectual concentration. Consider, for example, the doctrine of sin—surely one of the most badly understood ideas in the whole body of Christian teaching! By far the greater number of Christians throughout history (and still today!) have reduced the biblical concept of sin to moral wrongs and improprieties. Sins! We confess our sins. And with very rare exceptions the churches have simply accepted this reductionist conception of the biblical term; often enough they have not only accepted it but have *fostered* the misconception, for it contributed greatly to ecclesiastical power over believers. But in fact sin, biblically understood, is not first a matter of bad, evil deeds, or even the absence of goodness (sins of omission). Sin describes a condition of relationship—namely, of *broken* relationship. The doctrine of sin, which is closely associated with the biblical saga of the fall (Genesis 3), asserts that as human beings we are estranged from God, from one another, from the inarticulate creation, and even from ourselves. What is wrong with us is not that we "have done the things that we ought not to have done, and have left undone the things that we ought to have done."[8] It isn't a matter of *doing* at all, in the first place; it is a matter of *being*. Not that we *do* wrong, but that we *are* wrong: that is, at the center of our lives is a fundamental distortion. We are fallen creatures—fallen from the Creator's intention for us, fallen

8. The general prayer of confession in *The Book of Common Prayer*.

from our own faint residual knowledge of what we might have been. Our egocentrism manifests itself in broken relationships: alienation from all the counterparts of our being, whether in conscious and intentional estrangement or more subtly, perhaps mere indifference.[9]

The point, however, is this: our failure to grasp this profound anthropological analysis at the intellectual level, which is often more nearly a matter of stubborn resistance, usually conceals a problem with human nature greater than mere comprehension. We fail to comprehend sin intellectually because we resist—deeply, even fiercely!—the kind of spiritual or psychological truth that the doctrine wants to bring to our awareness. We resist the biblical conception of human fallenness because when it is articulated "existentially," it really does "explode existence" (Kierkegaard). As readers of Albert Camus's famous novel *The Fall* can testify, this kind of exposure to the dark side of human being and acting is profoundly unsettling.

In other words, the *kind* of thought that doctrine, sensitively presented and heard, asks of human beings is a thinking that goes well beyond the consideration of ideas and leads one into paths that may evoke a dark night of the soul. Not only the doctrine of sin and the fall, but *all* of the most foundational doctrines of the faith possess this *existential* thrust and demand. And if they do not—if they are presented merely at the level of "cleverness" (Kierkegaard) and received only at the level of an academic once removed—then they are not functioning as doctrine but only as matters of superficial interest. Unfortunately, just that is how doctrines have regularly functioned in the history of Christendom, and it is no wonder, in that case, that lay interest in them has dissipated in the modern period: ironically, a period that has seen the emergence of a burgeoning interest in the psychology of human relationships! We could pursue that observation as a failure of Christian apologetics; however, our present purpose is only to show that a prime reason for the complexity of Christian doctrine is that at its most authentic, doctrine intends to address the deepest recesses of human life. At least as seriously as Freudian and other modern forms of human analysis, Christian doctrine, when it is not simply doctrinaire, wants

9. In fact, sin as indifference toward others and apathy in relation to the world and to life generally, one of the most important themes in contemporary literature (e.g., Elie Wiesel's *The Town beyond the Wall*), has rarely been treated hamartiologically, because Christians have been too fixated on active immorality. Where theologians have ventured into the darker waters of sin relationally conceived, they have concentrated chiefly on pride; but sloth, which includes indifference and apathy, is perhaps more nearly the condition of humanity today.

to burrow beneath our consciousness and our practiced habits of suppression and repression, to the point where "truth in the inward parts" (Psalm 51:6, KJV) must be confronted. And that, as we all realize subconsciously if not consciously, is a very good reason for resisting . . . doctrine.

DOCTRINE IN RELIGION AND IN FAITH

Doctrine is necessary, in Christianity, because the gospel addresses the human mind; and that is hard enough. But Christian doctrine is made more complex still because the gospel intends to address—and heal!—the human soul; and that is the labor of a lifetime.

What we must now proceed to notice, however, is the qualitative difference that is made when doctrine ceases to be part of the "burden" (Tillich) of religion and occurs within the matrix of faith.

1. Doctrine and Religion

The Christian religion, like all systems of meaning, not only implies the necessity of doctrine, as we have seen, but it implies as well the continuous recall and rehearsal of doctrine within the religious community; for doctrine is nothing more nor less than the shared belief of the community. For its continuance, the community needs to remind itself often of what holds it together and enables it to engage in a common mission. Through study of the Scriptures; through conversation and discussion concerning the character of the *Zeitgeist* and the major instabilities of the age; through sermon and catechism and classroom; through common worship, prayer, and sacraments—in such ways the religious community nurtures its belief and maintains its unity of being and purposing. That unity should not and must not imply uniformity. The body must, and can, make room for a great variety of individual needs and individual gifts: that is the genius of the oneness sought by Christian doctrine, namely, that it does not spurn individuality but fosters it and gives it a place where it can fulfil itself in the context of mutual acceptance and comfort.

This recall and nurture of the doctrinal foundations of the religious community, however it may be undertaken, is essential to the life and mission of the community, for, as the Matthean metaphor of the wheat and the tares (Matthew 13:24–30) graphically illustrates, much in the life of the religious community, as indeed in most human communities, militates against the fragile quest for communality and undermines even the best approximations of the same. There is a necessary and lively dialectic involved in the concept of one body and many members; and when one or the other of these two polarities is allowed to dominate, the consequences can be devastating. If the corporate side of the dialectic is overstressed, individuals find themselves smothered by the tyranny of the group and the flowering of their gifts is lost to the community; on the other hand, when individual determination and initiative is permitted to go its way unchecked, dissension, malcontent, and the formation of parties and cliques easily leads to the breakdown of the community. Everyone who has experienced church life at any depth knows well these pitfalls! The only way in which the delicate balance between the group and the individual can be sustained is through regular recollection and discussion of the theological foundations of the community—that is to say, its basic *doctrine*.

The indispensability of such doctrinal discourse and discipline is demonstrated negatively by the experience of Christian churches and denominations that have neglected or shunned it. I have had at last to recognize, unfortunately, that my own denomination is a case in point. The United Church of Canada was formed less than a century ago, in 1925, when after much discussion and planning all the Methodists and Congregationalists and two-thirds of the Presbyterians in Canada determined to come together in one church. It was the first major church union in the North American Protestantism, and as a result the United Church became the largest Protestant denomination in Canada. Its future seemed assured, and many felt that the new church had combined the best qualities of its three denominational components: the piety and moral consciousness of the Methodists (the largest group), the importance of the local congregation (Congregationalism), and the doctrinal depth and seriousness of the Reformed tradition (Presbyterianism).

From the beginning, however, some criticism of the union was expressed, especially from the Reformed side; and one-third of the Canadian Presbyterians stayed out of the union. Their motivation for doing so was not as pure as many continuing Presbyterian apologists tried to maintain. The fact is that, in a strange and un-Presbyterian manner, the final decision about the union was left to individual congregations. Having grown up in a small village with only two churches (United Church and Presbyterian!), I can attest concretely to the fact that doctrine had very little to do with the Presbyterian congregations' decision not to unite, *or* the Methodist congregations' decision to do so! It is true, however, that some theologically astute and concerned Presbyterians[10] in the denomination at large feared from the start that the union had been inspired more by historical and cultural influences than by a serious, biblically based, and doctrinally considered ecumenism. It occurred, after all, at a time when the consequences of ethnic, national, and other types of societal divisiveness had been amply demonstrated by an outburst of human pride and mutual mistrust more devastating than anything in previous history: the Great War! The need to guard against such enmity, tribalism, and inevitable violence was felt by sensitive human beings in every walk of life. It was out of this cauldron that many different attempts at human reconciliation and mutuality were born, including the League of Nations, various peace movements, the labor union movement, and (in its pre–World War II beginnings) the World Council of Churches itself. It is legitimate to ask, therefore, whether the United Church of Canada was also inspired chiefly by this war-evoked recognition of the destructive potential of human separateness, suspicion, and disjunction. Did the new denomination emerge out of cultural idealism, and was its scriptural and theological basis merely rhetorical—perhaps even a matter of afterthought?

I have never been prepared to side with those (even among respected teachers) who faulted the union of 1925 for its doctrinal deficiency. I know that many thoughtful and well-informed Christians led the campaign for church union out of sincere conviction and Christian ecumenical hope. The *problem* of the United Church of Canada lies not, I think, in its beginnings but in its failure in subsequent decades to make good the *theological* as well as the social-ethical promise of those beginnings. John Coleman Bennett,[11] who was born in Canada and always manifested a particular interest in our country (rare among Americans!), frequently spoke admiringly of the fact that in the United Church of Canada the two prongs of basic Christian concern were united in one important administrative branch of the General Council: The Board of Evangelism and Social Service. I believe that this imaginative administrative combination of theology and ethics really did help to keep the denomination's attention focused on the theological basis of its life and mission, and to prevent ethics from becoming ontologically

10. For example James D. Smart.

11. Theologian, ethicist, and former president of Union Theological Seminary in New York City.

foundationless.[12] But the pull of the ethical side of the dialectic was predictably strong, partly no doubt on account of the majority Methodist influence in the Union; and since about 1960 that dimension, greatly affected by the various hot issues and causes that have dominated our social context, has flourished—and at the same time as doctrinal concern has diminished. For reasons that are very subtle and must await subsequent analysis, questions of basic belief have become increasingly problematic during the past half century, and in some ways it has been natural for the United Church of Canada, along with other liberal or moderate religious communities in North America and beyond, to turn more and more toward the ethical (and more specifically the *social*-ethical) component of the tradition, and to leave serious doctrinal discussion and concern to minorities within the denomination—the most vociferous among them, unfortunately, avowedly conservative or plainly reactionary groupings.

It is not surprising, therefore, that many now whisper, or even speak openly, about the quite-possible demise of the denomination. In the May issue of the *United Church Observer,* Patricia Clarke writes:

> with half of [United] church members over 65, and only 18 percent under 50, will there be enough people in the pews by 2025 to support that structure? For everything there is a season, a time to be born and a time to die. For the United Church of Canada, the time to be born was 1925. Perhaps by 2025 it will be the time to die, to be replaced by some new form of Christian witness.[13]

I have introduced this reference to my own denomination (though I realized that my discussion here would have to be extremely limited) because it illustrates very concretely the situation that has been developing throughout the remnants of classical Protestantism, at least in North America, and in fact the experience of the United Church of Canada may be regarded as a cautionary tale; for most of the liberal and moderate denominations of both northern countries on this continent manifest similar symptoms of decline, and the Canadian situation is in some important respects advanced beyond the US-American ecclesiastical context. In Canada, for instance, the *official* multiculturalism of the country has not only increased the actual presence of non-Christian religious communities,

12. See chapter 4 (below).

13. Patricia Clarke, "The Relationship between Congregations and the General Council Is . . . Frayed," Finish This Sentence, *United Church Observer*, October 2012. Online: http://www.ucobserver.org/opinion/2012/04/02/relationship/print/.

but it has probed very deeply and critically the old (Christendom) assumption that Christianity is the historical and almost natural character of our nation. Even in Quebec, though it has experienced in recent years a nearly militant secularism fueled by resentment of and revolution against the past hegemony of Catholicism, there is a new and nervous consciousness of Islam and other heretofore unfamiliar religions; and this combination of the loss of the patrimonial religious tradition and confrontation by true-believing forms of other faiths has produced the kind of cultural agitation that may be observed in many European countries (especially France), but that is not yet quite so evident in the United States.

In many ways the contemporary religious situation in Canada betokens a conspicuous failure of doctrine. The older forms of Christianity have heretofore been able to subsist—and sometimes even to flourish—for the simple reason that they have been part of the general cultural heritage. Doctrinal nurture and theological sensitivity were not really necessary to their continued existence. It could be assumed that generation after generation would make its way into the Christian church. One said that this had *always* happened! Four or five decades ago, when youth began to disappear from the pews, it was regularly remarked that "they'll come back, just as soon as they've had their fling and find themselves responsible for families." But in fact, as Patricia Clarke's observation ("only 18 percent [are] under 50") again demonstrates, large numbers have not come back, and most of them together with far too many who do continue to go to church, are almost completely at a loss to understand (let alone to articulate) what Christianity is all about! The complexity of Christian doctrine has in fact become, in these latter decades, a matter of utter confusion, when it is not a subject of sheer uninterest.

What we should read in this situation, however, is not only the failure of the churches to tend and nurture the theological roots of their belief. That, of course, is true—and obvious. But what is less obvious in this drama is the role of the underlying fact of its dominantly *religious* background. What we have been calling Christianity should be called, rather, the Christian religion. It is the Christian religion with which, with exceptions, most of us have been concerned. Where doctrine has been a prominent dimension of Christian denominations, it has been in the service chiefly of the sustenance and promotion of the Christian religion, represented by this or that particular ecclesiastical communion. And if in other denominations (like my own) doctrine has become optional, it is mainly because the Christian religion, whose welfare has always been heavy laden with racial, national, ethnic, class, gender, and other identities and objectives distinguishable from the Christian faith, has in the modern period become increasingly less vital to Western society. The *doctrinal* apathy and ignorance visible in varying shades in most of the once-mainline Protestant churches of this continent is, in other words, a consequence not only of neglect on the part of church theological leadership; it is an inevitable result of the limitations and finally the actual or imminent disfunction or demise of *religion*.[14]

Had the Christian church through the centuries been more sensitive to the distinction between religion and faith, this failure would have caused little surprise. Doctrine within the ethos of religion, as we have seen, was always fraught with difficulty. For most Christians during the heyday of Christendom, minimal knowledge of, as well as assent to dogma was largely a matter of duty and as much social as religious indoctrination. Doctrine was in fact a major aspect of, to borow Tillich's term, the "burden" of religion. Generation after generation was obliged to assent to a modicum of doctrines; without such assent one was virtually barred from full inclusion in society. For a few, to be sure, the exploration of doctrine became a matter of personal curiosity and interest; but for the majority a rote knowledge of rudimentary Christian teaching, together with the observation of church ritual, was simply mandatory. I am not among those who would attribute all this to the sheer power of ecclesiastical authority. The religious impulse, as we have argued in the introduction,[15] is a basic human tendency. We are (in modern parlance) hardwired for religion. Authority, as always, knows how to take advantage of this drive, and how to become excessive and overbearing in the process! The responsibility for the burden of religion should not, however, be laid exclusively at the feet of the ecclesiastical authorities. That is much too simple an equation. The entire phenomenon of religion is inextricably bound up with the human need to achieve control and security against the future. What Barth knew as this "grasping" quality of the religious impulse is found, not only in religious authority structures, which exploit it, but in individual and corporate life generally. Human beings both as persons and as a species, are gripped by anxiety about the future: let us

14. One of the most frequently heard statements in and around churches today is some version of the confession, "I am not *religious*, but I *am* spiritual." This so-common sentiment, combined with more studied observations and surveys, should tell us something quite significant about our religious situation.

15. And as Karl Marx himself maintained! Unlike Lenin, Marx did not define religion as an opiate *for* the people but as the opiate *of* the people. There is a vast difference there.

build ourselves a city, and a tower with its top in the heavens, . . . lest we be scattered abroad" (Genesis 11:4, RSV). The pair in the Garden (Genesis 3) were tempted to eat the fruit of the tree of knowledge because they thought that such knowledge could protect them from the unknown terrors of the future—a sentiment that can still be heard, *mutatis mutandis,* from educators and others! Knowledge of doctrine—*correct* knowledge, *orthodox* knowledge, knowledge sanctioned by patriarchy—could seem to secure, for both persons and communities, a bulwark against the "slings and arrows of outrageous fortune." If not on earth, at least in heaven a safe haven would be found. To have such security, human beings in ages past were prepared to believe religious authorities in a way that today most people in allegedly advanced societies trust only scientific authorities. Heretofore, the Christian religion has been wonderfully dependent upon this religious impulse. And still today, wherever the Christian church busies itself with its own preservation, it is largely reliant upon this same religious impulse. But for large numbers of our contemporaries in the most economically successful nations of the planet this impulse is greatly diminished, mistrusted, or unexplored. I, for one, do not believe that the assumption that human beings are naturally religious (*homo religiosus*) is passe. Contrary to some interpreters of Bonhoeffer's last writings, I believe that the religious impulse in post-Christendom societies has simply found other gods (including Science!) in which to seek its salvation. The Christian religion in such societies is no longer a popular receptacle of such naïve hope, and the more Christianity is reduced to such components of itself as we are treating in this study (biblicism, moralism, doctrinalism, and so forth), the less appeal it has for a sophisticated secular clientele. Christian simplism and predictability, combined with the presence in our midst of many other religious and secular sources of meaning, leave the Christian religion increasingly bereft of its traditional constituency. Churches are constrained more and more to seek their continuance and growth through the promotion of goods that are not directly related to doctrine, and that may in fact suppress doctrine in order to enhance their appeal.

2. Doctrine and Faith

At least in North America, the decline of the Christian religion is almost universally experienced by Christian leadership and active laity as catastrophe. But it *could be considered an unprecedented opportunity.* I do not mean an opportunity for conspicuous church growth or so-called relevance. I mean, rather, an opportunity for *authenticity*—including the authenticity of doctrine. This opportunity may be taken up, however, only by Christian bodies that recognize the distinction between religion and faith, and order their communities and their missions accordingly.

As we have observed in the introduction and first chapter of this study, that distinction was articulated with utter clarity and almost unprecedented brilliance by the leading lights of the early twentieth-century Protestant struggle to renew and rethink Christian theology. Karl Barth found religion, from the biblical perspective, virtually a matter of apostasy; Paul Tillich described religion as the great burden from which Jesus as the Christ wished to free us. Bonhoeffer understood religion as humanity's Babel-quest for security and power, which results in complete alienation. And in his final communications with the world beyond his prison cell, Dietrich Bonhoeffer anticipated—perhaps a little prematurely, but with luminous insight—the advent of a nonreligious form of Christianity.

Whether such a postreligious Christianity has or has not begun to manifest itself is yet a matter of discernment and viewpoint; but it is entirely clear, I think, that serious Christians can no longer assume that the human religious impulse will (quite naturally!) find a home in the *Christian* religion. In other words, Christian realism today means knowing that we live and think and teach and preach and worship and work *after Christendom*.

What does this mean for Christian doctrine?

It means that we can no longer rely upon a background of special openness to the promulgation of Christian teaching. In truth, we must now assume that Christianity, having ruled the roost for so long in Western societies, beyond having no apologetic advantage, is conspicuously impeded by its own past, its own reputation (whether deserved or undeserved). The most au courant among our contemporaries, many of whom gladly confess that they are spiritual persons, have little interest in pursuing a religion whose reputation for past authoritarianism and present reputation for lack of depth has robbed it of whatever intellectual appeal it might have had at certain high points of its long history. The sheer neglect and dismissal of the most profound and scholarly expressions of Christian theology in recent history, combined with the popularity of the most reductionist, gauche, and widely disseminated forms of the Christian religion in history (especially in the United States) mean that serious concern for Christian doctrine must now consciously assume a nonreligious matrix and basis. Quite concretely this means the matrix and basis of faith.

In reality, this new situation is by no means new! Genuine doctrinal concern has *always* assumed a foundation in faith. And where that basis was lacking, Christian doctrine was *always* a shadow and mockery of itself. The very language of the doctrinal tradition pinpoints the heart of this deception; faith could mean two very different human responses to church dogma, signaled by two Latin terms: *assensus* and *fiducia. Assensus,* meaning assent to specific doctrinal propositions, has dominated the whole discussion of faith in Christendom—to the point that still today church-folk speak of being unable to believe in the inspiration of the Scriptures or the virgin birth or the immorality of the soul.[16] That faith has always involved dogma (teaching) and concepts (doctrines) is obvious, but that faith is assent to dogma and doctrine is false even by the standards of the most universal Christian creeds: both the Apostles' and the Nicene Creeds confess belief in God, Jesus Christ, the Holy Spirit—not belief that such affirmations as are made in the creeds concerning the divine Being are true. Faith, like all of the major subjects of biblical religion, is a relational term, and it means simply trust—*fiducia.* "I believe in God the Father Almighty," and so on, does *not* mean that one believes in the existence of God, that God must be regarded as Father, that he created everything, and so forth. All of this means, rather, I trust God the Father, Mother, Parent, Source of Life, and so on: God, in all God's knownness and unknowability, is the Presence in whom I place my faith, my hope, my life and future.

If and when faith thus understood is present, *then*—and only then, in sincerity and truth—may *doctrina* be considered; *then,* indeed, doctrine must be considered, and considered, not as a foreign element imposed upon the believer or the community of belief, but as an inherent and deeply felt need, an exercise of mind and heart that cannot be ignored or avoided! As Augustine stated the matter succinctly: *Credo ut intelligam*; I believe in order that I may understand; and he continued, unless I believed I should not understand!

Faith, therefore, is the essential, existential, and primary foundation of genuine doctrinal study, reflection, and dialogue. Doctrine, when it is genuine and sincere, is consequential and secondary. Theology, which is a dialogue between the received doctrinal tradition and the pressing realities of the present context, is a derivative and second-order labor of the

---

16. A propos the general confusion in the realm of Christian teaching, it is precisely the nonbiblical idea of the soul's immortality, not the biblical conception of the resurrection of the dead, that dominates church piety and the secular environs of the churches.

disciple community.[17] Theology is to the gospel what literary criticism is to literature. Doctrine must therefore never be promoted as if it were the very essence and substance of Christianity. The very existence of theology in anything but the pejorative sense is dependent upon faith. Where there is faith, there will be an inherent and insurmountable drive to doctrinal thought and struggle. *Fides quaerens intellectum,* wrote Anselm of Canterbury, and Karl Barth rightly insisted that *quaerens,* in this phrase, should be thought of as faith's "voracious desire" for understanding.[18] Doctrine, in the community of faith and in the faithful individual will then not be a discipline of (often reluctant or halfhearted!) assent imposed upon believers by external (or internal!) authority; it will be a necessary, natural, *and joyful*(!) consequence of faith. And because it is the offspring of faith, it will also tolerate faith's opposite—doubt. Not only will it tolerate doubt, but it will encourage and even demand that doubt come out of hiding and articulate itself openly; for faith, in distinction from sight (2 Corinthians 5:7)—i.e., religious certitude—*is* a dialogue with doubt.

Conclusion: The Future of Doctrine

In the post-Christendom situation, and as it becomes clearer that this entails not only the end of a fifteen-century-long Western Christian establishment but the end, as well, of our reliance upon the Christian religion, among "the remnant that remains" doctrinal clarity and theological perspicacity will become increasingly mandatory. Simply to survive, the church of the future will have to become utterly serious about theology. While this demand will no doubt always require the concentration and discipline of a professional minority who are called and gifted for that particular aspect of the church's life, theology will be seen more and more as the *sine qua non* of the entire body. Doctrine, and the concern for depth of understanding, will become the concern of all who will to claim membership in the disciple community. Fringe benefits of church membership will no longer prove a sufficient reason to remain. The questions, why do I believe, and what do we believe?—that is, questions of doctrine—will be perennially present in the discourse of the Christian community, never fully or finally answered, never passe.

17. See, e.g., Lindbeck, *The Nature of Doctrine,* 10–11.

18. Karl Barth, *Anselm: Fides Quaerens Intellectum,* Meridian Books, Living Age Books 39 (Cleveland: World, 1960), 24.

And precisely for that reason *doctrine in itself must not be allowed to become the primary preoccupation of the church.* If the only authentic and serious form of doctrinal concern and work is one that presupposes *faith*, as Augustine claimed, then the *primary* obligation of the church's leadership is not to promulgate doctrine but to promote and work for conditions within the church and its environs that are optimal for the kind of questioning and meditation that invokes in human beings the quest for that in which to place their ultimate trust. If we can depend upon biblical and traditional ecclesiastical experience without emulating the worst practices and by avoiding caricatures of these offices, then we may assume that scriptural familiarity and the offices of preaching and teaching will be as prominent—and hopefully more imaginatively pursued—in the future as in the past. For it remains true that "faith comes by hearing" (Romans 10:17). However it may be undertaken or achieved—and that will always be a matter of trial and error—it seems likely that faith will be evoked and nurtured by an always haphazard and imprecise discipline of speaking and listening, silence, and dialogue. But increasingly, I believe, the evocation and nurture of faith will require a far greater emphasis upon personal dialogue and small-group discourse than has been the case in many Christian churches heretofore, where public performance (including the always questionable spectacle of mass evangelism) has been accorded biblically unwarranted attention. The task of *mentoring*, which is increasingly spoken of in secular educational circles as well, will have to become a more vital aspect of Christian discipleship and evangelism.[19]

But however the seeds of faith are sown in the Christian movement of the next centuries, doctrine and the biblical, historical, and theological disciplines required for its pursuit will be what it has always been for the true church: a prominent and indispensable dimension of the body of Christ. Christianity is not doctrine; but as the scholarly activity of second-order reflection on the faith, doctrine is a vital and irreducible component of what is meant by the noun *Christianity*.

19. In my own experience, as in that of most other articulate Christians known to me, the most important component in one's coming to the point of earnest curiosity about the Christian faith has entailed personal discourse with a few others—among them, often, persons whose friendship and conversation inspired in those who were searching for meaning and worth a strong need to study and reflect upon Christian claims for themselves. Such *mentorship* needs to be more carefully considered by all who have concern for the future of this profound intellectual and spiritual faith tradition. In this connection, see my recent book, Hall, *The Messenger: Friendship, Faith, and Finding One's Way* (Eugene, OR: Cascade Books, 2011).

4

Not a System of Morality

...the good that I would I do not,
But the evil which I would not, that I do ...
O wretched man that I am!
Who shall deliver me from this body of death?

ROMANS 7:19, 24 (KJV)

"WHAT MUST I DO?"

"YOU WILL KNOW THEM by their fruits" said Jesus (Matthew 7:16, NRSV). It is certainly one of his most-quoted statements, and it is used, most often, to bolster the argument that what really matters in Christianity is neither faith nor theology but how we actually behave: ethics![1] I suppose that most of us draw upon that argument from time to time; I know that I do. But it can be very misleading. It can imply that Christianity *at base* is an ethic. Take away all the dogmatic balderdash and all the nuanced scriptural exegesis, and what you have left is a system of morality. A very comforting idea to many proudly practical people! But the thesis I want to put forward in this chapter is a decisive rejection of such a notion and procedure. It is this: *Despite the indispensability of ethics for Christian faith and life, Christianity cannot be rightly or adequately described as an ethic or system of morality;*

1. Although the saying is usually employed to show that right ethical practice (*ortho-praxy*) is the best test of right doctrine (*orthodoxy*)—and that is how I shall use it here, too—the scriptural context is primarily interested in true (as distinct from false) teaching. Genuine truth issues in genuine goodness, yes; but genuine goodness presupposes an orientation to truth.

moreover, whenever Christianity is reduced to ethics, it forfeits the profundity of its kerygmatic center, which is gospel and not law.

This is so extensive a topic that I know in advance that I shall not be able to do it justice in a single chapter. Therefore, instead of presenting my argument in discursive terms, I shall turn at once to a passage of Scripture that illustrates better than any purely theoretical discussion could do, the reason why Christianity cannot be defined adequately as an ethic. It is not my purpose to comment on this text in a detailed way; I offer it, rather, as a narrative representation of the thesis that I have just stated.

> As [Jesus] was setting out on a journey, a man ran up and knelt before him and asked, "Good Teacher, what must I do to inherit eternal life?" Jesus said to him, 'Why do you call me good? No one is good but God alone. You know the commandments: 'You shall not murder; You shall not commit adultery; You shall not steal; You shall not bear false witness; You shall not defraud; Honor your father and mother.'" He said to him, "Teacher, I have kept all these since my youth." Jesus, looking at him, loved him and said, "You lack one thing: go, sell what you own, and give the money to the poor; and you will have treasure in heaven; then come, follow me." When he heard this, he was shocked and went away grieving, for he had many possessions.
>
> Then Jesus looked around and said to his disciples, "How hard it will be for those who have wealth to enter the kingdom of God!" And the disciples were perplexed by these words . . . and said to one another, "Then who can be saved?" Jesus looked at them and said, "For mortals it is impossible, but not for God; for God all things are possible." (Mark 10:17–27, NRSV)

THE REDUCTION OF FAITH TO MORALITY

It seems to be the fate of religion that it regularly—perhaps inevitably—devolves into morality. Moreover, the vagaries of human nature being what they are, morality—even the best of it—regularly devolves into moralism. I have the impression, from what I do know of other religions, that this generalization could find favor among their most critical members and observers. I doubt that the tendency is confined to any one religious tradition. Since, however, I lack both sufficient knowledge and experience of faiths other than my own, I shall confine myself here to Christianity.

Christianity as it came to me in my childhood and adolescence was almost unrelievedly fixated on morality; and while I have encountered a few persons of my age whose experience of the church was more expansive, most of us who grew up in Protestant denominations in North America during the years prior to World War II, and perhaps right through to about 1960, were heavily indoctrinated with moral admonition. The perceptive among us might sense, through biblical readings and the occasional sermon, or by observing exceptional laypersons who seemed to rise above the general milieu, that Christianity was more than morality; yet the message that came through to most of us, I think, was that what was wanted of us was an unrelenting and vigilant renunciation of the very misdemeanors by which, especially by the time we were adolescents, we were most tempted: consuming alcoholic beverages, smoking, swearing, gambling, and (in stricter circles) card playing, dancing, and any number of other little vices—vices whose viciousness would scarcely occur to our children and grandchildren today. Sex, one may say with hindsight, was certainly an *underlying* concern of our ecclesiastical and other mentors, but in the prewar period it was rarely mentioned explicitly at the level of public discourse.[2] Consequently, this forbidden subject was probably all the more prominent at the level of personal experimentation and curiosity.

I remember well a sermon preached in about 1952 by an outspoken minister of our denomination who used the evening services of his large church in the university city where I lived to air controversial topics of current concern. This particular sermon was advertised under the titillating title, "Sex, the Powder Keg." The immense Akron-plan sanctuary of the church was packed that night, mainly with students from the university. I arrived a little late and had to sit on the pedestal of the baptismal font. At last the unmentionable sin—not homosexuality (oh, no!—not in 1952),

---

2. In today's society, where sex is our every other word, few realize that prior to the 1960s, matters sexual were seldom mentioned openly in polite company. One of the advantages of age (there are a few!) is that one has actually lived through earlier periods about which the bulk of the population has only theoretical or (more often) hearsay awareness. For instance, one of the glaring and recurrent anachronisms found in present-day literature, television, and films happens when the so-called *f*-word, meaning sexual intercourse, is used, sometimes copiously, in stories set in the 1930s and 40s. The truth is that apart from sailors, prisoners, and vulgar youths, we simply didn't use that word in public. I remember as a child of eleven or twelve using it once, almost by accident, at the dinnertable in our working-class home. There followed dead silence! Then I was sent from the table in deep disgrace.

just ordinary sex, if sex is ever ordinary!—was going to be discussed openly, and in church! The sermon presaged even greater things to come.

They came, those things, with the various so-called revolutions of the 1960s and early 1970s. The new morality, as its advocates dubbed it, was to my mind at least in two respects an advance over the old: first, it was more honest in its assumptions about where we actually lived and what actually enticed and disturbed us; and second, in its best expressions the new morality introduced social ethics into the mind of the church at the congregational level in a way that had not occurred previously, except for those influenced by the Social Gospel. The old morality, at least in its local expressions, had been notoriously personalistic. A few social reformers in the churches could denounce the corrupting captains of industry who profited from the liquor and tobacco trades; but what reached the Sunday school rooms and the pews of local congregations was a highly personalized morality of abstinence, complete with the usual rewards and punishments. The new morality named the problems and possibilities young and not-so-young people were in fact facing, liberating some of us from rather dreadful post-Victorian assumptions and anxieties, particularly in the realm of sexuality. But the new morality also, at its best, made many of us think about the social conditions that fostered questionable or dangerous personal behavior.

But it was still . . . morality. It may have presented Christianity as containing more thou-*shalts* than we had heard before or had dreamed possible: thou shalt do thine own thing, thou shalt be liberated, thou shalt enjoy, and so on. But it was still a moral code, a pattern of behavior whose observance would render one acceptable to one's most coveted peer group; and therefore it had its own subtly oppressive side—as those could testify who were not part of the milieu by whom and for whom it was fashioned, namely the young, bold, and beautiful of the middle classes.

And of course it created a powerful backlash, one whose deleterious effects we are all still feeling. The Moral Majority, founded by Jerry Falwell and others in 1979, ushered into the social-political arena of the United States (and, by the usual process of cultural spillover, also into Canada) a coalition of Christians who, first, had not worked together before and, second, had been rather dormant politically. Now this admixture of ultraconservative Protestants, Catholics, Fundamentalists, and others reintroduced with a vengeance most of the moral strictures that had been present in the earlier period; but, more important, they were successful in imposing their allegedly true-believing moral code on large segments of society. The Moral Majority was officially disbanded by its leadership in 1986, but its influence extends well beyond the seven-year period during which it was front-page news. The Moral Majority went very far in confirming, or reconfirming, the public impression that Christianity *is* at its heart a system of morality, and a very explicit one—one that presents (as the new *Encyclopedia of Protestantism* notes) a "political platform [that is] pro-life, pro-family, pro-moral, and pro-American, and that denounces abortion, pornography, homosexuality, and feminism."[3]

This thumbnail sketch of the near identification of Christianity with morality in our own immediate period is not unique, however contextually determined are its specifics. From its beginnings, Christianity manifested a tendency to devolve (and I shall explain presently why I think the word *devolve* should be used here) into morality. Already in the brief period of Jesus's ministry, the greatest pressure on Jesus, coming from his detractors as well as from some of his followers, was to produce clear-cut moral directives. This pressure is heard, with more than the usual sympathy, in the question of the rich ruler, who, at the most obvious level, hopes to find in Jesus a final, decisive, and persuasive answer to his question, "What must I *do*?" But, beneath the surface of his question, Jesus hears in this person a genuine plea for help. So the man distinguishes himself from most of the others who badger Jesus with their demands for moral certitude or tokens of adherence to religious law. "Looking at him, [Jesus] loved him," says Mark. I shall return to that thought later.

By the time we get to the second century of the Common Era, writings like the *Didache* tend to cast the whole faith of the Christians in the imperative mood, which, after the Gospels and the Epistles of Paul seems to many perceptive readers something of an anticlimax. With the establishment of Christianity in the fourth century, this seemingly unstoppable equation of Christian faith with moral rectitude and conformity is enhanced, and it is intensified by the need of civil authority to have its code of personal and public behavior strengthened and legitimized by the new official cultus. And if we had the time to follow the relations between Christianity and culture through these twenty centuries, we could easily document, I think, what most of us already assume, namely, the many ways the Christian religion became the bearer of the moral assumptions and systems of the

3. Seth Dowland, "Moral Majority," in *The Encylcopedia of Protestantism*, ed. Hans J. Hillerbrand (New York: Routledge, 2004), 3:1306–7.

successive empires, races, classes, and other dominant social forces with which the churches bound themselves, or by which they were bound.

WHY DOES THE MORAL DIMENSION DOMINATE?

The question is, why? I do not mean to ask why morality should be a fundamental concern of Christianity; I assume that it should be. But why, both historically and still today, should the *moral* dimension of this faith so consistently become the *dominant* one? Why, for vast numbers of human beings throughout the history of the church, should the adjective *Christian* connote—and connote *primarily*—a certain code of behavior, a certain set of moral assumptions? Why should such a statement as, *He's a good Christian man* regularly be understood to mean that he has a reputation for moral rectitude (in whatever way that may be understood in a given context), rather than (say) that he has a profound understanding of and belief in Christian teaching, or that he is a faithful member of a Christian congregation, or that he is a person of prayer, or any number of other things that could be said about him as a Christian?

Three conspicuous reasons seem to arise for this perennial identification of Christianity with morality: *First*, moral teachings and exhortations are more accessible than is the thought upon which profound moral reflection is based. "Human wisdom," said Luther, "is more inclined to understand the law of Moses, than the law of the gospel."[4] Not only in the case of Christianity, but in every religious and philosophic position of depth, moral reflection and ethical counsel are consequential. That is, they are grounded not only upon experience but, perhaps over centuries, upon discerning and critical thought about experience. They assume some depth of insight about what the ancients called the nature of things. An earnest quest for what is *good* may inspire an equally earnest search for what is real, essential, true; but until an ethic is understood to be consequential upon what is perceived to be real, essential, and true, it remains an arbitrary ethic, a moral system without ontological foundations and one, therefore, upheld—insofar as it *is* upheld—only by external authority or custom. *The Christian ethic* (if such a term is permissible, which I doubt)[5] is a consequence of what Christians

---

4. Thomas S. Kepler, ed. *The Table Talk of Martin Luther* (New York: World, 1952), 172.

5. In fact it is a highly presumptuous term, for it suggests an unchanging and untouchable moral agenda, whereas in fact authentic ethical behavior, Christianly

believe about the nature of things—the reality and presence of the divine, the redemptive work of God in the Christ, the providence of God in history, the vocation of humanity to responsibility within the sphere of creation, the mystery of the divine Spirit's internal testimony, the authority of Scripture, and so forth. In short, the Christian ethic is a consequence of the subject matter of Christian theology. Theology precedes ethics, not simply as an intellectual exercise, but as the continuous and deeply engaged quest of the Christian and the Christian community to understand and articulate what faith believes to be real, true, meaningful, and faithful—in common parlance, what is really 'going on.'

But it is extremely difficult to discover precisely what is really going on, because it requires both intellectual concentration and spiritual risk. Many people, however (to some degree, all of us!), resist any such descent into the depths of understanding. Thought is draining, and especially in a world like ours, whose great moral and physical problems demand not only time and devotion but the courage to confront very dark dimensions of reality. We want more readily available, less unsettling, counsel for our lives. As did the rich man in the scriptural incident, we want to know what to *do*. As everyone who has led a discussion on almost any topic in almost any North American church will attest, the very first question from the floor will likely be some version of precisely this rich man's question, but what can we do? And usually this question, in whatever specific form it is asked, functions as a way of terminating any further discussion of the problem under consideration. We do not like simply to suffer the problem, as someone insightfully put it. Let us have answers, and let us have them at once! Years ago I saw a poster on the wall of a Protestant meeting place, and I assumed immediately that it had got there by some mistake, for it read: "Don't just *do something, sit there!*" There is an enormous resistance in our activistic, quick-fix society to prolonged thought about anything requiring prolonged thought. We prefer to take the results of somebody else's thinking and make a show of applying them as we will or can—which means, in practice, not only that we are blown about by every trend, but that we compound the very problems we are presumed to be concerned about. Morality tends to dominate in religion, then, because it is easily reduced to exhortation and act; it is easily accessible.

---

understood, is always responsive to contextual realities that necessarily alter what, in faith, one *does* on account of new factors, problems, and possibilities within one's context.

Second, morality rises to the top because moral systems, and espe-cially those that discourage original, critical thought, always serve powerful vested interests. Such interests are present—and sometimes conspicuously present—in the Christian community itself, whose structures of authority benefit from the identification of the faith with moral assumptions requir-ing a modicum of reflection on the part of the membership. The tendency of religiously backed moral systems to bring about uniformity of behavior is of course augmented in the situation of religious establishment, whether legal or cultural, for then not only the ecclesiastical but also the secular authorities are served by the moral systems in question. The primacy of moral concern does indeed, as I've already suggested, show itself already in the New Testament; but with the establishment of Christianity preoccupa-tion of religious authority with morality became paramount.

To illustrate, once I was asked by a sex therapist on a television pro-gram why it was that the church had such narrow and restrictive views on human sexuality. "Was it Jesus who started all that?" she demanded. No, I assured her, it was not! Given the moral climate of his time and place, Jesus was in fact extraordinarily open and compassionate where human sexuality was concerned. He was far more concerned about the self-righteousness of those who drew attention to the sexual sins of others! As a religion, even in its preestablishment form, Christianity has rarely appeared as receptive and broadminded about matters sexual as was its Founder! But as soon as the Christian movement allowed itself to become the official cultus of a powerful civilization, it had to assume the mantle of a moral police force. Societies, particularly highly regulated ones, have always been especially wary of sexuality, because it really is indeed (for such societies) "the powder keg," the potentially chaotic element that will undo all the efforts of those who maintain order. Most of the stringency that is attributed to Christian sexual ethics should be traced, not to the original sources of the faith, but to social and political concerns of the imperial cultures with which Christian-ity has made its bed.

Third, however, we should not too quickly blame external causes for this premature and perennial identification of Christianity with moral sys-tems. There is clearly something very human about the quest for moral guidance. The *economically* secure man who came to Jesus was obviously *psychologically* insecure at a quite basic level of his existence. For all his pro-priety as a keeper of the commandments, he did not feel . . . right, genuine, at peace with himself. His moral accomplishments as one who had (pretty superficially, one supposes) observed some of the established laws of his tradition, served no more than did his material accumulations to satisfy his desire for inner calm. His quest is not (as the biblical language might suggest to *our* ears) a quest for fulfilment in some supernatural realm. The "eternal life" he seeks, because he does not feel he knows it or has it, concerns life here and now, not *only* then and there. He wants to be for real; he wants to have done with pretence and hypocrisy and superficial acceptability; he wants to feel acceptable within himself; he wants (to use a modern term) authenticity. And he feels—hopes!—that there may be some quite practical way of achieving that end—some moral directive, something that he can do to achieve such authenticity.

Such a quest for "purity of heart" (to use a Kierkegaardian term) is more common among us than cynics may think. No one can doubt—today!—that human beings are capable of very terrible things, even of great *wickedness*, a word no longer reserved for preachers of fire and brimstone but resorted to with considerable regularity by journalists. Yet there is also within most of us a sincere if inconsistent and intermittent and only half-formed desire to be good. St Paul speaks for most of us when he writes about "the good that I would . . . the good that I want to do . . . , the good person that I would like to be." Systems of morality are not merely imposed upon us by religious and other agencies that have vested interests in molding us; they also appeal to something within us. Indeed, if one is able to get behind some of the surface preoccupations of contemporary life, one is sometimes prone to think that the most pressing, if convoluted, yearning of our species is to discover how to be good. We obviously conceive of the good in a great many, often conflicting ways; but the quest for the good is stronger, I suggest, than is imagined by jaded intellectuals. Thus we give ourselves to an astonishing array of schemes and dreams and visions of the good life, few of them (no doubt) worthy of serious consideration, many of them illusory and ultimately demeaning, some of them downright dangerous; yet beneath them all rests a longing to be . . . other than we are.

So, in sum, morality is accessible; it is appealing to authority; and it speaks to basic needs in human nature. For all three of these reasons, not least of all the last, Christianity is under enormous pressure to present itself as a promoter and arbiter of moral rectitude—I will not say moral righteousness, because that kind of outmoded religious language would leave liberal Christianity out of account; and liberalism is at least as enticed by the demand for moral prescription as are the more conservative Christian groupings that can still be happy with a term like *moral righteousness*. The level of moral confusion and insecurity is so high in our social context that the preacher who can bring forth from sources old and new clear moral directives, and do so with panache (and perhaps with the help of a battery of electronic gadgetry and popular musical entertainment) will not lack for a congregation. Few among the hearers of such preachers will notice that the dominant if not the exclusive linguistic mood of their sermons and addresses is the imperative mood—*must* and *should* and *ought **to***, because most congregations will be listening precisely for just such specificity: the kind of concrete moral advice that the rich man of the biblical text, at the most immediate level of his consciousness, thought that he wanted and needed.

THE LIMITATIONS OF MORAL EXHORTATION

But when the Christian church gives in to this demand for straightforward moral exhortation, it betrays both its own message and vocation and the human beings for whom its message is intended! It's as simple as that!

I do not mean that the church should shun moral counsel, whether personal or social. Obviously that is not an option for a faith that is shaped by its world commitment and its hope for individual life. But when morality and moral admonition, however sound, necessary, or sophisticated, becomes the chief and perhaps the exclusive concern of a Christian community, that community (I repeat) will have betrayed both its own message and vocation, and the human beings for whom its message is intended.

Let us consider the latter first: how does such a resort to moral exhortation betray humanity? In answer, we return to the biblical story: at the most obvious level, we said, what the rich man wants (or thinks he wants) from Jesus is precisely moral direction. He wants—or seems to want, or thinks that he should want—to be told straightforwardly, *This* is what you have to do. If you want to be good; if you want life without any hint of failure or guilt or lingering self-doubt; if you want peace of mind and spiritual blessedness, here's what you must do! But Jesus, who has already been alerted to the superficiality of this reading of the situation by the man's effusive salutation, "Good teacher," knows how ultimately meaningless it would be to respond as though he were glad to play the role of the good teacher, the exponent of higher morality, the guru of how-to.

The man's response to Jesus's next comment confirms the impression Jesus has of him from the outset: here is a person who has maintained throughout his adult life most of the principal regulations of his religion—but only externally and without troubling himself overmuch with questions about the motivation for his seeming obedience. And, as we know from the Sermon on the Mount and elsewhere, it is human motivation and intention that interests Jesus particularly—because that is where the great spiritual struggle of men and women takes place. You may not have committed adultery or done murder (good for you!), but have you looked at another with lust or felt hatred for another in your heart? And what does all your self-conscious observation of these laws signify for you in terms of your self-estimate: are you not exceptionally well-pleased with your law-abidingness, your moral superiority? Do you not take infinitely more pride in your alleged goodness than in anything else, even your possessions? How often have you in fact done "the right thing for the wrong reason" (as T. S. Eliot puts it in *Murder in the Cathedral*)? Have you considered how basically egotistical it may have been for you to make a project, a lifework, of moral self-improvement? Are you not, even now, wanting me—the good teacher to put the finishing touches to your lifelong preoccupation with self?

Here is another observation about this text: It is interesting that the commandments the man assures Jesus he has kept "since his youth onwards" are all of them commandments that *could* be kept by conscientious religious observers, and often have been—so far as external observance goes. Interestingly, the commandment against covetousness, which cannot be objectivized, is not included. Nor is the very first commandment: "I am the LORD thy God, thou shalt have no other gods before me" (Exodus 20:2, KJV). Who can stand before *that* commandment? Of it Luther said, "I have many times essayed thoroughly to investigate the Ten Commandments, but at the very outset, 'I am the Lord thy God,' I stuck fast; that very one word, I, put me to a *non-plus*."[6] The biblical commandments are not moral instruction, to be abstracted from the divine–human encounter that is their basis and their context. The presence of the I who utters them—this Eternal Thou in whose sight and hearing they are to be lived out—this changes everything about them!

We are told that Jesus "looked upon" the rich man and "loved him." One could pause for a long time on that. I suggest it means, at least in part, that Jesus's compassion for this man—a compassion he did not feel for the

6. Kepler, ed. *The Table Talk of Martin Luther*, 8.

self-righteous scribes and Pharisees who so often dogged his steps—has something to do with Jesus's recognition of the pathetic combination of underdeveloped self-knowledge and genuine longing for authenticity that he sensed in this particular human being. What the rich man needed, he recognized, was not another exhortation to moral rectitude but a radical reorientation, a profound awakening to the realities of his own and the world's condition: in biblical language, *metanoia*, a word that is usually translated as "repentance"; but that too is a term spoiled by its own religious history. It really means being turned around completely, transformed, set on a different path, changed from within. Jesus's final advice to the rich man, therefore, is not to be heard as yet another moral directive—"Go and help the poor!"—but rather as a highly perceptive and profound word of spiritual counsel. This man, he knew, would only attain the peace he sought if he could *forget himself sufficiently, become sufficiently nonchalant about both his material wealth and his naïve self-righteousness, to enter fully into life*. Life! It is life, not religion, that Jesus wants to give us, says Bonhoeffer. This might happen to him, Jesus believed, were he to become newly aware of the suffering of his contemporaries. He had within him, Jesus obviously believed, the potential for what Simone Weil called *attention*—perhaps even for compassion, solidarity, selfless love; or rather, this potentiality lay not within him, not simply as his, this man's, possibility, but (as Jesus said later to his disciples) a potentiality that was God's possibility for him.

I have spoken concretely of this particular scriptural figure, this rich man; but I have done so because he is, I think, so transparently representative of the biblical reading of the human condition generally—and at its best! That conception is not unaware of our terrible pride and egotism; yet it sees in our *superbia*, our *hubris*, a pathetic bid for a meaning we fear we do not have; it is not unaware of our guilt, but it sees in our incipient consciousness of guilt a desperate desire for purity; it is not unaware of our evil, but it sees in our distaste for conspicuous wickedness an unquenchable memory of the good for which we were created. It is a betrayal of this human potentiality for "truth in the inward parts" (Jeremiah 31:33) when, instead of testifying to the possibility of realizing or approximating that potentiality, which is always *God's* possibility and gift, religion burdens humankind by adding to the oppressive moral agenda that we place upon ourselves and one another still more demands, allegedly emanating from sacred sources.

NEITHER RELIGION NOR MORALITY, BUT *LIFE*

But when the church allows itself to become the purveyor of morality, it betrays not only this deep and hidden humanity that is asking for life (for 'salvation,' if you like), it also betrays its own message and mission. For what the community of the Christ has to offer humankind is neither a new religion nor a new code of behavior but newness of life. "I came," said Jesus, "that they might have life, and have it abundantly" (John 10:10). When it is true to its calling, the primary vocation of the church is not to exhort or cajole or threaten people into *doing* something, but to offer them a way of becoming and of *being* something—something, someone, different, changed, renewed, and able to begin again. Only out of this new *being* will radically new attitudes, practices, and deeds be born—deeds that are not only externally right but motivated by generosity, compassion, justice, love.

It is lamentable, surely, that so much of the Bible's own language for this kind of transformation has been rendered practically useless for serious Christians on this continent. It has been taken over, lock, stock, and barrel, by certain well-known forms and groupings and styles of being Christian, which have rendered it all but inaccessible to serious persons outside and inside the churches who try to be honest about their own life and experience and—so far as they can claim it—religious faith! Nevertheless, we cannot get around it: the New Testament not only uses the language of rebirth, but it assumes that what this language signifies is the condition without which ethical discussion remains at the level of arbitrary, imposed imperatives—*must, should, really ought to.* Something (shall we call it sin?—another badly scarred religious word!)—*something* impedes our best intentions to do "the good that we would"; something draws us again and again to the old, selfish me-first-ism that colors even our best deeds, even our loves. This something has to be changed, and radically, according to biblical faith; and, distasteful as it may be in a social context where one-third of the population of allegedly the most Christian (and most aggressive) nation on earth claims that status, one of the metaphors the gospels use for that radical change is rebirth.

In an incident recorded by the writer of John's gospel—the visit with Jesus by night on the part of one, Nicodemus (an account that may be traced to the same oral source as the Markan account I have used here), Jesus tells the rich man (now actually named Nicodemus), "Very truly, I tell you, no one can see the kingdom of God without being born from above" (3:3, NRSV) or "born anew" (RSV). Everything in the New Testament (and much in the Old)[7] points to this same sense of the necessity of a new beginning, a radical transformation. It is assumed that humankind in its present state is unable or unwilling (likely both!) to rise above its self-absorption sufficiently to be the creature its Creator intends—the creature it, itself, somehow remembers and longs to be. And what is that? It is a creaturehood conscious of and concerned for the well-being of the other. It is a creaturehood sufficiently liberated from self to begin to notice, care about, feel for, identify with, simply *see* the world through the eyes of . . . the other: the other who is God, the other who is neighbor, the other (and we must say this often today) that is the extrahuman creation. The whole intention of the law, the divine Commandment, according to both Jesus and Paul, is to make entirely clear and obvious what God intends for this strange and perhaps impossible creature called the human. The entire purpose and vocation of this creature, the Bible affirms, reduced to its most foundational, is simply this: *to love*—to love the other. All of this creature's other undoubtedly noteworthy and even unique capabilities (its astonishing capacity to think, to reason, to contemplate; its ability to exercise a power of will, its adaptability, even its manual dexterity), all these endowments, according to the testimony of Jerusalem (which in this respect particularly differs from Athens) are given this creature for one, overweening purpose: to love!

But if this is the Bible's first and most basic assumption about this creature, its second is that, alas, under the conditions of existence, it is precisely this creature's capacity to love that has not been realized—and, apparently, cannot be realized by divine imperative, exhortation, moral directive, law. Love, the mind and heart of the Christian ethic, cannot be achieved by commandment; yet only love—of God, of the neighbor, of the world and its myriad creatures and processes—can make any profound difference to the state of humanity and the fate of the world. Therefore, since the biblical God seems stubbornly unwilling to let the creation self-destruct, the only alternative stratagem biblical faith contemplates involves a radical transformation of this problematic yet key figure in its story, the figure who is the antagonist, or perhaps the protagonist, of its drama:

"You must be born anew . . . born from above . . . born again!" This presents us, in the liberal and moderate churches of North America, with an enormous dilemma. How can we use this language, or even language like it,

---

7. Here is a sterling example: Jeremiah 31:31–32: "Behold, the days are coming, says the Lord, when I will make a new covenant with the house of Israel . . . I will put my law within them, and I will write it upon their hearts."

in a religious and cultural milieu where this language has been co-opted by a powerful and numerous segment that has been able to commend itself to large numbers of our population who, though not part of itself, are almost ready to believe that real Christianity lies precisely in that direction? How can we use this language, or even language like it, when so many Americans declare themselves—without the least embarrassment or pain—to be born-again Christians, and whose Christianity is manifested most conspicuously, not only in an extraordinary kind of national and personal self-satisfaction, but in an imperialistic behavior among the nations and peoples of the planet? How can we use this language, or language reminiscent of it, when it has come to signify very stylized and, to many of us, gauche and crass religious attitudes; and when this highly self-promotional piety of the born-again appears to make so little difference in its adherents' *collective* consciousness of the great suffering of the greater share of our planet, of both its human and its extrahuman inhabitants; when, on the contrary, this same super-Christian religiosity strengthens and enhances the very economic, political, racial, military, anthropocentric, and other dimensions of the global status quo that cause and sustain this suffering?

This is not a theoretical dilemma for serious Christians in North America today; it is very basic. The language of radical human transformation, which is indispensable and foundational for the whole biblical message, has in so many and such obvious ways been taken over by forms and manifestations of religion abhorrent both to secular sensitivity and to the more sober and informed remnants of Protestant, Catholic, and Orthodox Christianity that these remnants find it difficult to articulate what is most foundational to our common theological heritage. Even the term *gospel* has been colored by this powerful, media-conscious segment of the modern church. We old-line Protestants hardly know how to use it any more! We shy away from anything that smacks of evangelicalism, and thus puts us at a disadvantage with the classes and institutions that have been our social mainstay.[8] The language of radical transformation was always incommensurate with our respectability in the forms of establishment that we enjoyed in the past; and today, in our evident progress toward complete disestablishment, we find ourselves nervous about any recovery of that language on account of its association with the fundamentalist, ultra-evangelical, and morally restrictive versions of our faith with which we cannot identify.

8. See my recent book, Hall, *Waiting for Gospel: An Appeal to the Dispirited Remnants of Protestant "Establishment"* (Eugene, OR: Cascade Books, 2012).

At the same time, the most thoughtful, engaged, and responsible persons and groups among our own once-established churches have been alerted to some of the most pressing ethical problems ever to have threatened human civilization and creaturely survival: a burgeoning human population, most of which lives in poverty and illness; profound injustice at the level of race, gender, and material well-being; a deteriorating environment under the impact of a technological mindset that refuses limits; violence and civilizational enmity, most of it either caused or accompanied by religious bravado, ignorance, and intolerance. Earnestly, desperately often, those most conscious of these life-threatening conditions cry out for change, for radically new policies on the part particularly of the possessing peoples of the earth, for human rights and the rule of reason and law, and serious international concern for the fate of the earth.

Like many who will read these words, I like to think myself a member of that company. I am convinced that true morality in this time and place would simply have to lead in that direction. I believe very firmly that the only *ethic* that could claim any legitimate connection with Jesus Christ today would have to be (in the words of the 1988 General Assembly of the World Council of Churches, meeting here in Vancouver) an ethic stressing "justice, peace, and the integrity of creation."

GOSPEL, NOT LAW

But I am also convinced, as a Christian, that such an ethic cannot be achieved merely as an ethic, as moral imperative, even (in the words of my revered mentor, John Coleman Bennett) as radical moral imperative.[9] The very changes that our best and most humanly responsible voices are calling for today—profoundly radical changes; changes not only in human behavior but in the very way we think, desire, hope, and plan: these changes cannot be brought about merely by shouting about them or by holding international conferences or even by threatening what will occur if they are not implemented.

And the demand for change at this truly abysmal level is being least heard and most resisted by the possessing people of the planet. By us! We—the economically, technologically resource-rich and militarily powerful nations of Earth—we collectively are the rich man of this scriptural story.

9. See John C. Bennett, *The Radical Imperative: From Theology to Social Ethics* (Philadelphia: Westminster, 1975).

It fits us almost to a T. Our possessions are great. Our religion—whether it be some remnant of traditional religions or the new religions of consumerism and tourism and entertainment makes little difference—has rendered us spiritually smug. Yet we are covertly fearful and even (in Kierkegaard's sense) *despairing*, with the despair that does not and will not admit itself to be despair. For we have discovered . . . death. Finitude. Mortality. Limit. End.

For some—I think them a chosen few—Jesus's counsel to the rich man that he abandon his possessions and seek out the poor will be, has been, the means of their transformation, as it was for St. Francis, for Mother Teresa, for Simone Weil. Not a few in our time, in fact, have been changed conspicuously by their solidarity with those who suffer most, whether in Latin or Central America or Africa or Indonesia, or here in our nearly ungovernable megacities. Yet the majority, I suspect, will be like the rich man of this Scripture and turn away from such counsel saddened; for the moral counsel itself cannot transform.

And the question that this analysis leaves for those of us who still feel bound to this ancient tradition of Jerusalem, and who still ponder the legacy of classical Protestantism—the question beneath all the questions—is this: How shall we recover *gospel* in such a time as this? How shall we articulate God's possibility for a humanity that has begun to know, at a deeply hidden and disturbing level of consciousness, something of its own impossibility? We have seen—at least the most engaged of us have seen, with a new clarity—that moral imperatives will not suffice for such a world as has come to be. The very changes that our most debilitating problems require—the demand for justice, for peace, for creational sensitivity and respect—can scarcely be touched by even the most passionate and informed moral exhortation. For they require a transformation of mind, spirit, and body so vast that it seems impossible for human beings—especially for us, the rich. How then can we speak meaningfully today of *God's* possibility? The possibility of grace, of repentance, of spiritual renewal and hope—yes, of *rebirth*?

This, I have come to believe, is the great challenge and test to which, today and tomorrow, serious Christians are being put: Can we get beyond our worn-out and, at base, boring reputation for moral exhortation—law? Can we articulate *gospel*—or something worthy of that biblical term?[10] Can

---

10. See my recent book, *Waiting for Gospel: An Appeal to the Dispirited Remnants of Protestant "Establishment"* (Eugene, OR.: Cascade Books, 2012).

we proclaim a message of transformation and hope that is beyond doing? Can we discern an indicative, a givenness or reality, that can undergird and make real and credible the truly radical imperative that planetary life now demands? Can we testify to a transcendent love that could lay claim to us in our confused and needy humanity, and engender within us some echo of its own great generosity?

There is no general, once-for-all answer to these questions. But, as the story of the rich Nicodemus makes so wonderfully clear: *God's possibility* opens out before us whenever and wherever we know that we are at the end of our own possibilities.

5

Not the Church

"Many whom God has, the Church does not have;
and many whom the Church has, God does not have."

<small>AUGUSTINE[1]</small>

THE NECESSITY OF THE CHURCH

LIKE THE BIBLE AND Christian ethics, the church is clearly a vital aspect of what the noun *Christianity* connotes. Christianity without the church is possible in theory and *perhaps,* under certain circumstances, in practice (one thinks of the No-Church movement in Japan, for instance).[2] While the term *church*[3] may certainly suggest an element of the accidental or ar-

---

1. *De Baptismo,* 5.38.

2. The No-Church movement stems from Uchimura Kanzo (b. 1861). He was converted by Methodist missionaries at age sixteen and educated at Amherst College. He wrote: "Christianity minus churches is the Way, the Truth, and the Life. There is no reason for leaving Christ and his Gospel because churches which are its institutional vestments are soiled and odious. Churchless Christianity will be the Christianity of the future. The seer of Patmos said: 'I saw no temple there' (Rev. xxi.22)." *Selected Works of Uchimura Kanzo* (Tokyo: Iwanami, 1953), 298.

3. Luther clearly did not like the word "church" [*Kirche*]: "If these words had been used in the Creed: 'I believe that there is a holy Christian people,' it would have been easy to avoid all the misery that has come in with this blind, obscure word 'church'; for the term 'Christian, holy people' would have brought along with it, clearly and powerfully, both understanding and judgement on the question 'What is and what is not a church?' . . . But because we use this blind word 'church' in the Creed, the common man thinks of the stone house, which we call a church, and so painters depict it; or if things turn out better, they paint the apostles, the disciples, and the Mother of God, as on Pentecost, with

bitrary, it remains that any body of persons intentionally gathered around the teachings, memory, or felt presence of Jesus Christ and the people out of whose long history he emerged functions as a church no matter what it may be called.[4]

And precisely as such the church is a vital aspect of what Christianity is all about. For it is of the essence of this faith that the hearing of the Christian message, the gospel, brings together and unites persons separated from one another by sin, that is, by indifferent, broken, or destructive relationships. Out of many, the Spirit of God intends to create a unity—one body—, and this is not tangential to the evangel but its provisional goal. The New Testament certainly knows about *individual* conversions—that of Saul of Tarsus (Acts 9) being the most prominent; but far from stressing individual conversions as though they were themselves the goal (in the manner, for example, of much North American evangelism), the New Testament gospels and epistles see them as part of or means to a greater end. That greater end includes the church, though as I shall argue presently, it also goes well beyond the church. The whole Christian message or *kerygma* (proclamation) is reflected in the coming to be of a community of discipleship, which embodies the basic elements of the evangel: the forgiveness of sin, the breaking down of barriers between persons and peoples, and the heralding of a new situation in which mutuality triumphs over egoism, peace over hostility, sharing over greed, compassion over vindictiveness and revenge, and so on. While the church cannot claim to *be,* in any full sense of the term, that new creation, it nevertheless participates in the kingdom or reign of God announced by the gospel that it is called to proclaim. It is itself the first consequence of the *kerygma.* It is the *necessary* consequence of the

the Holy Ghost hovering over them." Hugh Thomson Kerr, ed. *A Compend of Luther's Theology* (Philadelphia: Westminster, 1943), 125.

4. The word *church* itself is an old English word with equivalents in other European languages (*kirk,* Scottish; *kerk,* Dutch; *Kirche,* German), all of them derived from the Greek *kuriakon,* meaning the dwelling place of the lord (*kyrios*); but the Greek word does not appear in the New Testament. It should go without saying (though perhaps this always needs to be said!) that the habit of using the word *church* to refer to buildings and ecclesiastical properties is *not* biblical, though it is easy to see how such a habit came to be, given the characteristic human tendency to associate places with their uses (bank, school, parliament, for example). Christians during the early period did not have their own buildings; they met in the homes of members or in public places, sometimes hidden from public concourse, such as the famous catacombs of Rome. When, in English translation of the Scriptures, we read the word "church," therefore, we should assume that it normally translates another Greek term, *ecclesia,* meaning an assembly of people who believe themselves to be called together by a common message and mission.

Christian message because without it the message itself would be so abstract as to appear mere theory and quite literally unbelievable. A message of reconciliation is credible only when it is proclaimed by a community of reconciliation. Thus the church, in whatever language it may describe itself, is certainly prominent in the scriptural and traditional understanding of what *Christianity* ought to mean.

This is borne out by the scriptural text usually regarded as depicting the inauguration of the church: the second chapter of the book of Acts.

> When the day of Pentecost had come, they were all together in one place. And suddenly from heaven there came a sound like the rush of a violent wind, and it filled the entire house where they were sitting. Divided tongues, as of fire, appeared among them, and a tongue rested on each of them. All of them were filled with the Holy Spirit and began to speak in other languages as the Spirit gave them ability. (vv. 2:1–4, NRSV)

The narrator resorts to the language of spectacle in order to convey the truly miraculous thing that he believed was happening on that occasion—which was *not* the sound and light show, the fire and wind, but rather the fact that diverse, culturally and linguistically divided human groupings were brought together by the hearing of a message that both judged and revived them, a gospel that broke down "dividing walls of hostility" (Ephesians 2:12, RSV). That message, so far as it could be put into words, is articulated by the Apostle Peter, following immediately upon the Pentecost experience as a kind of explanation of what was happening. But the narrator's point is that Peter's words are only able to move his hearers so profoundly because of a transcendent power that the words in themselves do not possess. It is this power—the power of the divine Spirit—that brings about both the *speaking* and the *hearing* that creates the church:

> And at this sound the crowd gathered and was bewildered, because each one heard them speaking in the native language of each. Amazed and astonished, they asked, 'Are not these who are speaking Galileans? And how is it that we hear, each of us, in our own native language . . . ? (Acts 2:6–8)
>
> So those who welcomed [Peter's] message were baptized, and that day about three thousand persons were added. They devoted themselves to the apostles' teaching and fellowship, to the breaking of bread and prayers. (2:41–42, NRSV)

Scripturally and doctrinally speaking, then, it is to be understood that the church, as the creation of the Holy Spirit—the Third Person of the Holy Trinity—is integral to the very purposing or providence of God. To speak of Christianity is to speak of the church.

THE CHURCH AS MEANS TO A GREATER END

But is the church all that Christianity means? When we have explored the central significance of the church for this faith, have we exhausted the meaning of *Christianity*? Is Christianity synonymous with the church or the churches? Do Christians think of their faith as a faith that is fully embodied in the churches and inseparable from them—perhaps even from one of them in particular? If a well-informed Christian wished to explain Christianity to non-Christians, would he or she be justified in assuming that this could be achieved through acquainting the non-Christians with an actual body of Christians? Supposing not only one but many churches were explored by the non-Christians, and at depth: would such an exercise suffice to define Christianity?

Few Christians, even among those who have a very high doctrine of the church, would wish to answer these questions straightforwardly in the affirmative.[5] While Christianity and the church are inseparable both historically and theologically, they are not synonymous. Christianity remains the larger and church the smaller category. Christianity, as a way of naming the *faith* of the church, always transcends the church as such. The church, when it is earnest and faithful, always hopes to manifest or even embody Christianity, but when they are honest, churches know perfectly well that they fall far short of what true Christianity would have to mean. For one thing, they always embody other realities besides Christianity—for example national, ethnic, racial, cultural, or broadly historical or ideological realities that never belong absolutely to Christianity and that often enough must be judged *un-Christian* or even *anti*-Christian. When G. K. Chesterton in a famous dictum asserted that Christianity had not been "tried and found wanting" but only "seldom *tried*," he was not exempting

---

5. Those who argue that the church is the extension of the incarnation may want to differ here; Protestantism, however, does not go that route. The encyclical *Mystici Corporis Christi*, issued June 29, 1943, by Pope Pius XII, accentuates so entirely the principle of identification in the relation between Christ and the Church that it is begs the question whether Christ's being *head* of the *body* (Paul's metaphor) is not compromised.

the churches from the critique implied in this generalization.[6] They too—
and perhaps even *especially* they—fall short of the reality that is signified by
the term, Christianity.

Besides embodying cultural specifics not of the essence of Christianity, the church in its historical sojourn has embodied another phenomenon
that, as we have seen in the introductory chapter of this study, biblical
thought regards with considerable suspicion: religion! We noted that religion in the Scriptures and in the work of many recent theologians connotes
the human attempt to *grasp* after and if possible control ultimate power or
deity. The myth of the Tower of Babel (Genesis 11), as Bonhoeffer and others have taught, describes this temptation symbolically. Pentecost reverses
this orientation: it depicts the gracious movement of God toward humankind. In other words, at least so far as its origins are concerned, Christianity
did not understand itself as a religion but as a response to God's initiating
grace—a community of *faith*, a people "called out" (*ekklesia*). However, as
Karl Barth insisted, "historic Christianity itself is religion, and must constantly come under the criticism of the Gospel."[7] There is perhaps more
Babel than Pentecost in empirical Christianity! It would not be altogether
wrong, even though it would be one sided, to say that the history of the
church has been a series of various *corruptions* of Christianity, some of
them spectacular!

The other side of such a generalization, however, makes it necessary
for us to add that Christians have been rather more prepared than are many
other historic religions to engage in an ongoing critique of itself, even to the
point (in contrast to Islam, for instance) of using humor and satire to draw
attention to "the judgment [that begins] with the household of God" (1
Peter 4:17, RSV). From the seven letters of the Spirit to the churches of Asia
Minor (Revelation 2–3) to Søren Kierkegaard's *Attack upon Christendom*,
Christians and churches have been, on the whole, unusually conscious of
their own shortcomings. It belongs to their confession of sin, an essential
aspect of their public worship: "We have left undone the things that we
ought to have done, and we have done the things that we ought not to have
done, and *there is no health in us.*"[8]

---

6. See A. N. Wilson, *Tolstoy*, Classic Biography (London: Penguin, 1988), 337.

7. Helmut Gollwitzer, *Karl Barth's Church Dogmatics: Selections*, trans. G. W. Bromiley (Edinburgh: T. & T. Clark, 1961), 50.

8. *The Book of Common Prayer*, general confession of sin.

Christians' hesitation to identify Christianity with the church is due not only, however, to their realization that the church falls short of truly Christian expectation and behavior. It is also—and more positively—because the church's *mission* presupposes an end far greater than itself. The community called together by the Spirit of Pentecost is made to understand from the outset that it is not the *ultimate* object of the good news by which it has been gathered together. It is in fact more means than end. The gospel contains an inherent necessity: it must be shared. Indeed, the very existence of the church, with its unique quality of unity in diversity, is for the sake of its limitless *mission*. The church is incomplete in itself. Its vocation takes it far beyond its own borders. "The church is her true self only when she exists for humanity."[9] Such a mission demands on the part of the church, a new and radical orientation towards the world (*cosmos*); for, as that most familiar of scriptural texts, John 3:16, asserts, it is *the world* that God "so loved" in Jesus Christ. When the church behaves as though it were in itself and exclusively the object of God's electing love, it betrays its purpose in a flagrant manner. As Jesus prays (according to the Gospel of John), "As you [Father] have sent me into the world, so I have sent them [the disciples] into the world . . . I ask not only on behalf of these [the first community of discipleship] but also on behalf of those who will believe in me through their word, that they may all be one. As you, Father, are in me and I am in you, may they also be in us, so that the world may believe" (John 17:18–21, NRSV).

That the early church remembered this teaching (what we may call the subordination of its existence to its mission) is evidenced not only in the acts of the martyrs, who were ready to give up their own lives for the sake of the message and Way they had to proclaim; it is also clearly preserved in Christian doctrine, specifically so in the Nicene Creed's marks of the church. The first three traditional marks (or *notae*) named by the Creed— "one, holy, catholic"[10]—do indeed stress the importance to faith of the church itself: its unity, its set-apartness (holiness), and its universal, supranational (catholic) character belong to the core of the Christian confession. But the fourth mark—*apostolicity*—contains an implicit but radical critique of the notion that the existence of the "one, holy, catholic" church is the goal of the God of the New Testament. The church is a people *brought together*

---

9. Dietrich Bonhoeffer, *Letters and Papers from Prison* (London: SCM, 1953), 180

10. The marks or notes of the church (*notae ecclesae*) as codified in the so-called Nicene Creed.

in order to be *sent out* into the world, as the so-called Great Commission of Jesus at the end of the Gospel according to Matthew makes clear: "'*Go therefore and make disciples of all nations . . .*'" (28:19). The Creed's three previously-named *notae* provide the necessary foundation for this fourth, missional mark. The church that does not hear and enact this fourth characteristic of its being, the church that is content to be an institution rather than a people on the move (*in via*) is a church that has fallen into temptation—the temptation of all human organizations that become fixated upon their own well-being.

Ironically, though not surprisingly, it is just this temptation that has plagued the history of the church and has been its peculiar hubris. The most deeply rooted philosophic antecedents of this temptation are not to be found in the traditions of Judaism, though historical Judaism has always been tempted by this same hubris; but the *ideational* background of the temptation must be traced to a certain recurrent theme in the philosophic and religious traditions of Athens, namely, the idea of an elite. That idea is very far from the concept of divine *election* in both the older and the newer Testaments. Jerusalem and Athens do indeed share an assumption, which like all assumptions may of course be questioned by others: the assumption, namely, that among the great masses of humanity only a few in all probability, will grasp the deeper significance of reality. As Elizabeth Barrett Browning put it poetically—

> Earth's crammed with heaven,
> And every common bush afire with God,
> But only he who sees takes off his shoes;
> The rest sit round and pluck blackberries.[11]

While Athens and Jerusalem share this (perhaps melancholy) thought that there will only be a few, there is an enormous difference between the conclusions drawn from this common assumption. Typically, for Athens (the Hellenistic world), the few are thought of as the goal toward which all history strives.[12] For Jerusalem, on the contrary, the few exist for the sake of the (blackberry-eating!) many. The elect are not a golden minority who have risen above "the herd" (Nietzsche!); they are not a select coterie who live on another, higher plane of being. Rather, for the tradition of Jerusalem the few are (yes!) *chosen*—but chosen for a purpose infinitely more gener-

---

11. Elizabeth Barrett Browning, from *Aurora Leigh*.

12. One has this, for instance, in gnosticism.

ous and expansive than their own being and destiny. They are chosen as witnesses to a new reality intended for all.

This distinction is absolutely vital to a biblically based conception of the church. Far too often in the history of Christianity, the biblical concept of election has been interpreted as though it were yet another version of elitist thinking. Indeed, it would not be an exaggeration to say that every major ecclesiastical grouping—Catholic, Protestant, Orthodox; evangelical, liberal, even Unitarian Universalist!—has at some time or other, if not perennially, fallen into the habit of identifying *itself* as specially, perhaps exclusively, favored by the divine Source, or, in the more secular groups, by history. This exceptionalism, as it is sometimes called, is nothing more than a form of elitism; it is to be differentiated quite strictly from the biblical concept of divine election.

Election, in the scriptural understanding, is beautifully interpreted in a remarkable sermon of the great Karl Barth—a Reformed theologian who strongly defended the doctrine of election, though he was critical of Calvinistic idea of double predestination.[13] Barth's sermon is titled simply "All!" It is based on the Pauline text, "For God has made all men prisoners, that he may have mercy upon all" (Romans 11:32). Given the wording of that particular text, it is not irrelevant to note that the *context* in which the sermon was preached (on September 22, 1957) was *the Basel prison.*[14] As the sermon's title already announces, Barth effectively repudiates all the elitist connotations, whether ecclesiastical or political, that the doctrine of divine election has been caused by unthinking or deliberate chauvinism to bear.

> We must start with the fact that God had mercy and will have mercy on *all*—that his will and work are determined and governed by compassion . . .
> . . . God says 'yes' to us, he wills to be on our side, to be our God against all odds . . .
> Contrary to human mercy even in its kindest expression, God's mercy is almighty . . . We do not need to be afraid that it might be limited or have strings attached

---

13. I.e., the notion that some are predestined for salvation, others for damnation.

14. As is the case with all of the sermons in the collection called *Deliverance to the Captives,* trans. Marguerite Wieser (1961; reprinted, Eugene, OR: Wipf & Stock, 2010). The sermon, titled "All!" is found on pages 75–84.

Let us pause here for a moment. As according to God's holy word, spoken in Jesus Christ, he has mercy on all, each one of you may repeat . . . 'I am one of them.' . . . The one great sin for anyone right now would be to think: 'This is not meant for me. God does not have mercy on me . . .'

But wait a minute! Because according to the word that God has spoken in Jesus Christ he has mercy on all, we may and must repeat in our hearts: 'Among all people on whom God has mercy are this man and that woman, this fellow-creature beside me, in front of me or behind, whom I don't like to remember. . . . The one great sin from which we shall try to escape this morning is to exclude anyone from the 'yes' of God's mercy . . .

The text insists that God has made *all* [people] prisoners of disobedience. *All*, including me, the preacher of this Sunday sermon? Yes, including me! . . .

. . . this is our common predicament, none shall secretly exempt himself; none shall point to the other fellow as a more obvious target; none shall think of himself as an exception. . . .

God's purpose [however] is not to debase us nor to put us to shame. . . . [Rather] He places us on the very spot where his mercy is operative and manifest.

FAITH BEYOND THE PALE?

The hint of universalism implied in Barth's sermon[15] anticipates a question that must now be addressed explicitly. If the compassion of God is extended to all, must we think that it is extended only through the auspices of the church? May we not suppose that intimations of this grace will be found also *outside the church*?[16] And in that case is it not possible that something anticipatory of Christianity, or at least not antithetical to it, could be observed outside the bounds of communities that consciously and intentionally define themselves as Christians?

---

15. To be sure, Barth himself shied away from the idea of universal salvation. He felt that such a concept too easily devolved into a spiritual ideology or law, calling into question the freedom of the God to "be who I will be."

16. Barth, as is well known, did not pursue this line of thought. With his emphasis upon the centrality and sufficiency of revelation, he mistrusted the more apologetic emphasis of Emil Brunner, who thought that human beings, even in their separation from and rebellion against God, manifest a certain capacity for God (*capax Dei*). At least they are addressible.

The suggestion that Christianity transcends the church, and that its expression outside the church is sometimes more luminous than what transpires within, cannot be dismissed as a product of cynicism about the empirical church or of indiscriminate theological liberalism. Its antecedents are much too deeply rooted in the tradition for that. Indeed, they run like a leitmotiv throughout Christian and Judaic history. They are clearly present in the New Testament, where they echo a theme frequently aired in the prophetic literature of the Hebrew Scriptures. In the older Testament, the tendency of "the chosen" to regard their election as a privileged *status* rather than a vocation to representative service and suffering is continuously condemned by the prophets as presumption and vainglory:

> You only have I known
> of all the families of the earth;
> therefore I will punish you
> for all your iniquities. (Amos 3:2, RSV)

The prophet Isaiah even dares to name notorious enemies of Israel as God's own people, and "blessed" as such:

> In that day, Israel will be the third
> with Egypt and Assyria, a blessing in the
> midst of the earth, whom the Lord of
> hosts has blessed, saying, 'Blessed be
> Egypt my people and Israel the work
> of my hands, and Israel my heritage. (19:24–25, RSV)

This same astonishing readiness to find God's work and God's people well beyond the bounds of religious assumptions and prejudices is powerfully expressed at the very threshold of the New Testament's story, when John the Baptist, the herald of the Christ, turns upon Pharisees and Sadducees who have approached him for baptism and shouts: "'You brood of vipers! Who warned you to flee from the wrath to come? Bear fruit that befits repentance, and do not presume to say to yourselves, 'We have Abraham as our father'; for I tell you, God is able from these stones to raise up children to Abraham." (Matthew 3:7–9, RSV). Reputation, credentials, membership rolls, and all such paraphernalia of belonging are not what counts, and in fact they regularly deceive both their claimants and outside observers. As we noted in the previous chapter, Jesus picks up this same theme in the seventh chapter of Matthew, where he contrasts external marks of belonging with the only authentic test of identity as Christian—which is actual behavior: "You will know them by their fruits" (Matthew 7:16, NRSV). It is generally assumed that this refers to moral or ethical behavior; but it should not be confined to ethics. The fruits of faith are not only good works but also a sincere and sustained search for understanding, orientation toward truth, discernment of signs of the times, courage to hope, and above all, as Paul insists in 1 Corinthians 13, the spirit of love. False, hypocritical, or merely nominal Christianity are not sound trees from which good fruit is to be expected; they are like bad trees that should be "cut down and thrown into the fire". "A sound tree cannot bear evil fruit, nor can a bad tree bear good fruit" (Matthew 7:18, RSV). To use other terms, *authentic* Christian faith generates behavior that is good, not because *we* are especially good, but because there is at work within us a primal goodness that transcends our egoism. The fruits are "fruits *of the Spirit*"—which the Scriptures variously identify as "goodness" (Ephesians 5:9), "righteousness" (Philippians 1:11), "peace" (James 3:18), "love" and "joy" (Galatians 5:22).

Nothing guarantees that such authentic Christianity will always be found in the church; nor does anything guarantee that such behavior will *not* be found outside the church! If what calls itself Christian is frequently not the real thing, the obverse should also be seriously considered: i.e., that the real thing may also be found among those who make no claim to Christian identity! Even, perhaps, among the avowedly non- or even anti-Christians!

That possibility is indeed made quite explicit in the theology of St. Matthew. Immediately following the words we have just quoted concerning good and bad trees and their fruits, Matthew has Jesus remind the faithful that the mouthing of pious language and the claims of membership in Christ's flock guarantee nothing about Christian authenticity:

> Not everyone who says to me, "Lord, Lord," shall enter the kingdom of heaven, but he who does the will of my Father who is in heaven. On that day many will say to me, "Lord, Lord, did we not prophesy in your name; and cast out demons in your name, and do many mighty works in your name." And then will I declare to them, "I never knew you; depart from me you evildoers." (7:21–23, RSV)

By the end of his gospel, however, Matthew speaks explicitly of this *other*, even more disarming aspect of the distinction between appearance and reality: namely, the astonishing fact that without any connections, credentials, or other accoutrements of membership in the *soma Christou* (body of

Christ), some complete outsiders are bidden by the One they never knew as "Lord"—and in the most welcoming terms!—to "inherit the kingdom prepared for you from the foundation of the world" (Matthew 25:34, RSV)!

This remains, surely, one of the most truly *radical* passages of the newer Testament. While it would be ridiculous to exaggerate the comparison by claiming that the officially religious are simply rejected, it is not possible to *avoid* the fact that the chosen ones are depicted in this passage as being not only ignorant of the Lord but also quite unconscious of their own goodness. Apparently, like persons who "don't let their left hand know what their right hand is doing" (cf. Matthew 6:3), they simply saw what needed to be done, and did it! There was no particular reward for them in doing it, because those to and for whom they did it were not important figures but "the least"—the bottom of the heap: the hungry, the parched, the naked, the sick, the imprisoned, and so forth.

The stark radicality of this teaching leaves none of us untouched. In the face of the parable of Matthew chapter 25, we especially who *are*, in some sense of the term, members of the church in good standing cannot help feeling judged and found wanting. *As we undoubtedly are!* But those who are made most uncomfortable by this shocking New Testament text are those who have so circumscribed belonging that they cannot entertain the thought that some whom their ecclesiology blatantly and a priori excludes may have priority in God's sight over those who profess belief. "Truly I tell you," cried Jesus to the priests and elders whose spiritual *securitas* made them question every outsider, beginning with Jesus himself, "tax collectors and prostitutes are going into the kingdom of God ahead of you" (Matthew 21:31, NRSV).

EXTRA ECCLESIAM NULLA SALUS

The sheer unprotectedness of such a conception of Christianity, combined with the actual experience of confusion, dissension, and fragmentation within the Christian movement as it expanded into the ancient Mediterranean multiculture, is undoubtedly what lay behind the early Catholic teaching, *extra ecclesiam nulla salus* (outside the church there is no salvation). This teaching dates back to the third century CE. The *movement* character of the early church—the church as the people of the Way, *communio viatorum*—was giving way swiftly and increasingly to institutionalization and the need to define more explicitly the boundaries of Christianity.

With the beginnings of Christian *establishment* under Constantine and his successors, definition inevitably became even more mandatory. The very purpose of Christianity, as conceived by its new imperial protectors, was bound up with the potential of this religion for fashioning out of great cultural diversity a unity of belief and purpose sufficiently profound to overcome the tendency of human collectives to revert to tribalism, polytheism, warfare, and political chaos. Imperial Rome was on the verge of disintegration. Christianity, whose unique monotheism[17] was able to absorb or at least tolerate difference, seemed ideally suited to stem, if not wholly to reverse, the breakup of the impressive empire that Augustus and his armies and engineers had achieved. But if Christianity itself were to capitulate to the territorial and doctrinal divisions already threatening to destroy the church's own unity, it would be necessary for the policymakers of church and society to become far more explicit about the boundaries of Christian belonging than had been the case heretofore. It is not accidental, therefore, that the most significant public act of the Emperor Constantine following his proclamation of religious toleration[18] was to convene an ecumenical gathering of Christian leaders, the purpose of which was to end serious doctrinal division and state in explicit (creedal) terms what the designation *Christian* must and should mean.

This concern for definition and boundaries persisted throughout the ages of Christian establishment. The Reformation was of course a profound challenge to this concern; but even Protestants, as they encountered

---

17. Not all monotheism lends itself to the toleration of difference. In practice, and especially where it has been bound up with secular power, Christian monotheism, like that of Islam, tends to require of its adherents strict obedience to the One God (as interpreted by both religious and secular authorities). In part, the fourth-century struggle of the stricter monotheistic parties against the dangers of tritheism was inspired by the religious and political desire for uniformity and by the fear that diversity courts chaos. Biblical monotheism, however, honors dialogue and diversity. While insisting on the unity of the Godhead, it also insists on the integrity of the human spirit. Believers appear before the One God with awe and reverence, but also in all honesty—ready, if need be, to struggle with God, to give voice to their doubt, to ask for reasons, to question. Such a dialogical/dialectical conception of the divine/human relationship is reflected in the human-to-human relationships that characterize the church.

18. The so-called Edict of Milan (313 CE) ended for the time being state persecution of the Christians. While it did not establish the Christian religion as the favored religion of Rome, it should be seen as a step in that direction. The completion of the process did not occur, at the level of the state, until the reign of Theodosius the Great (379–395 CE). With the convocation of the Council of Nicaea in 325 CE, however, Constantine virtually declared himself in favor of something like Christian establishment.

threatening divisions within their own ranks, made use of the *Extra eccle-siam nulla sallus* principle. No one should be greatly surprised at this need for definition; it is perennial. Today, in the *post*-establishment situation of the Christian religion, it is still necessary to ask about the limits within which the term *Christianity* may be meaningfully employed; otherwise, the designation becomes so fragmented or vague that in the end it means everything and nothing. This is not a theoretical danger in the present context in North America. It is all too real in ultraliberal religious circles where diversity and inclusivity of outlook trumps any concern for scriptural and doctrinal specificity that might (*horribile dictu!*) prove to offend or exclude some. In this climate not only doctrinal specificity but even the study of doctrine—even theology itself!—can seem suspect of a certain narrowness of outlook. In consequence, Christianity in these contexts tends to be a matter of consensus: an article of belief is true, or at least acceptable, if a majority of the members and adherents of that church or denomination assents to it. Thus in and around the edges of the liberal churches one observes a state of enormous confusion and constant flux.. For many, *Christian* and *Christianity* connote little more than a vaguely moral or attitudinal condition. Large numbers of persons in post-Christendom societies still attach a certain value to these terms and are ready to tell census takers and other inquirers that they are Christian (they may even name a particular denomination); who, even in our blatantly secular society, wants to be thought un-Christian? But many have little or no knowledge of the Scriptures or traditions that bequeathed the Christian religion to us. A church that no longer asks about its theological foundations will be absorbed, sooner or later, into the general secular *melange*. It is only a matter of time.

The dilemma therefore may be stated as follows: D*efinition, including the setting of boundaries, is essential to any spiritual community that wants to have a future; but, unfortunately, definition is regularly much too successful!* There are pitfalls on both sides of this dilemma. Ultraliberal Christians, wishing to appeal to the broadest possible cross-section of their social context and unwilling to define themselves for fear of exclusivity, court ultimate absorption and extinction; ultraconservatives, fearful of losing their identity, define themselves in increasingly extreme (fundamentalist or legalist) terms and are reduced to ghettos—though some (in the United States particularly) are politically powerful ghettos.

Given this dilemma, reflective and responsible Christians must learn how to define their faith in such a way that the term *Christianity* does *stand for something specific,* yet recognizes that this is a faith whose boundaries are porous enough to take account of that *beyond themselves* that reflects or approximates or at least does not wholly contradict the gospel, though it does not identify itself as Christian.

WHO KNOWS?—
ECCLESIA VISIBILIS/ECCLESIA INVISIBILIS

We can be helped toward the development of such an ecclesiology by pondering in the light of present realities ecclesiological traditions that have not been accorded a very imaginative hearing among the most prominent institutional expressions of Christianity. One such tradition is the Protestant distinction between the visible and the invisible church—a distinction that many believe can be traced to Augustine of Hippo.

It fell to Augustine to sort out a controversy that had arisen in the wake of the persecution of Christians under Emperor Diocletian in 303–304 CE. During this fearful episode, some Christians had—in the view of certain purists in North Africa headed by a bishop, Donatus Magnus—compromised their faith by fleeing the persecutors or offering tokens of their loyalty to the imperium. When the persecution had subsided, the question was of course whether these turncoats (*traditores*) could now in any way be accepted again into the fold. The so-called Donatists were adamant: they could not. Augustine, ever conscious of his own history of disobedience and of the undeserved grace of God, argued against this rigorous (one might say puritanical) conception of Christian belonging; and in this connection, in his treatise on baptism, composed the sentence that I have placed at the head of this chapter.[19] Whether or not Augustine's provocative distinction represents the actual roots of the visible/invisible concept, it certainly stems from the same basic mentality.

It was inevitable, in any case, that the chief sixteenth-century Reformers should draw upon that approach, for it was implicit in their profound skepticism about the authenticity of the papal church. Significantly, however, they did not wholly dispense with this skepticism when considering the various churches that grew out of their reform. They were too well schooled in Scripture to imagine that the new Protestant churches could ever claim

19. Hendrikus Berkhof translates Augustine's Latin somewhat differently: "Many who seem to be without are in reality within, and many who seem to be within yet really are without" (*De Baptismo,* 398).

unquestioned authenticity or finality. The true church—the company of the Elect, in Calvin's terms—is known only to God. It is the creation of the Holy Spirit. It cannot be ascertained by human beings, however learned or authoritative. One believes—one *hopes,* one acts as though!—the true church is found also among the membership of the church visible. But no human being or ecclesiastical body can *identify or name* those who have truly been touched and transformed by the *testimonium Spiritus sancti internum. Internum!* Who has seen the wind? Who can trace the unpredictable course of the divine *Pneuma?*[20] Who can discern the inner thoughts and loyalties of the human heart? God alone knows who, among all those who *claim* belonging, truly belongs to the body of Christ. Of the *visible* church Calvin writes:

> In this Church are included many hypocrites, who have nothing of Christ but name and appearance; many persons ambitious, avaricious, envious, slanderous, and dissolute in their lives, who are tolerated for a time, either because they cannot be convicted by a legitimate process, or because discipline is not always maintained with sufficient vigour.

Nevertheless, Calvin insisted that this visible church must be taken seriously: "As it is necessary therefore to believe that Church, which is invisible to us, and known to God alone, so this Church, which is visible to men, we are commanded to honour, and to maintain communion with it."[21] Without forgetting that "the true members of Christ" are known only to God, Christians are thus required to believe that "wherever we find the word of God purely preached and heard, and the sacraments administered according to the institution of Christ, there, it is not to be doubted, is a Church of God."[22]

---

20. *Pneuma,* the Greek word from which such English terms as *pneumonia* and *pneumatic* are derived, means "wind" or "breath" and, by extension, "spirit" or "soul." The Holy Spirit is the divine wind or breath that breathes life into matter.

21. *Institutes of the Christian Religion,* trans. John Allen (Philadelphia: Presbyterian Board of Christian Education, 1936), book 4, chapter 1, article 7.

22. Ibid., article 8. Karl Barth follows Calvin in this insistence that the *visible* church has to be taken with great seriousness. "Take good note, that a parson who does not believe that in this congregation of his, including those men and women, old wives and children, Christ's own congregation exists, does not believe at all in the existence of the Church. *Credo ecclesiam* means that I believe that here, at this place, in this visible assembly, the work of the Holy Spirit takes place." Barth, *Dogmatics in Outline,* trans. G. T. Thomson (London: SCM, 1949), 145.

This handling of Calvin's "two senses" in which the term *church* is used illustrates clearly the dialectical manner in which the major Reformers approached this subject. While they were utterly realistic about the admixture of "wheat and tares"[23] in the visible church, they did not want the idea of the invisible church to function as a rationale for cynicism or neglect with respect to the visible church.

That delicate balance—some would say juggling act!—was barely honored, however, by some of the most significant Protestant movements of subsequent centuries. From the mid-seventeenth century onwards, the existence of *Protestant* forms of establishment (state churches), which manifested both a rationalistic approach to theology (Protestant Orthodoxy) and a lack of sincere spiritual conviction, evoked protesting elements within Protestantism itself. The most important of these were various expressions of what came to be known as Pietism.

Beginning with Philip Jakob Spener (1635–1705), a Lutheran, Christian thinkers deeply concerned about the laxity, spiritual indifference, and corruption of European Christendom attempted to renew and enliven the churches by activating Luther's teaching concerning the priesthood of all believers. They encouraged the development of groups of sincere believers *within* the (visible) church, which, through Bible study, prayer, the discussion of sermons, and other such projects might serve to bring new life to congregations whose faith had grown rote or apathetic. These *ecclesiolae in ecclesia* (little churches within the church) belong to the long tradition of attempts on the part of engaged Christians to purify, renew, or reform larger politically or culturally recognized Christian bodies. In the English-speaking world, the life and work of John Wesley illustrates poignantly (and rather successfully!) just this approach. Wesley, an Anglican priest, had no desire to break with the Church of England; but in the end his pious critique could not be tolerated by the established Church or contained within it. Most of the Christian denominations in the North American context today can be traced, in one way or another, to this same pattern of purification, rejection, and separation.

It is easy enough to show that all such efforts to reform the church visible court fallacies and dangers on the opposite side of this equation—self-righteousness, fanaticism, division, and so forth; but it should also be noted that in the absence of such a questioning of ecclesiastical authenticity (*simper reformanda!*), Christianity lacks not only clarity of purpose

23. See Matthew 13.

but also credibility. By definition, *discipleship* is not an option for serious followers of the Christ. And discipleship is never satisfied by a merely statistical membership in the *visible* church.

Hendrikus Berkhof questions whether the visible/invisible distinction of earlier Protestantism still has validity.

> An "invisible church" is a contradiction in terms . . . Naturally the church, just as for that matter any human institution, has a visible outside and an invisible inside: faith, hope and love are as such invisible. But the fact that not all church members are believers is a truth which as such is not an ecclesiological concern. The centuries-old problem is more sociological than theological in character. Now that the Constantinian era is coming to an end and the churches everywhere are becoming voluntary, the problem is losing its urgency. We see now that the theologians dreamed of the invisible church as fulfilling all those desires that could not be realized in national churches.[24]

Professor Berkhof's opinion, it seems to me, may be more pertinent to the European context, where Christian establishment took for centuries the form of legally designated state churches, than it is to the situation the United States, Canada, Australia, New Zealand and elsewhere, where the establishment of Christianity has been cultural and informal—though not, for that reason, less significant. The ending of the Constantinian era, which is a major historical phenomenon occurring irregularly and over a long period of time, is much less conspicuous in our context (especially in the United States) than in Europe. Besides, even where the process of disestablishement is widespread and obvious, serious Christians still are—and always will be—faced with the question of authenticity: what does *genuine* Christianity look like, or at least what does it *not* look like?

There is, however, another way in which the visible/invisible distinction may be a significant, *usable* tradition upon which Christians today could draw—whether in the clearly disestablished situation or in the "awkwardly intermediate stage of having once been culturally established but . . . not yet clearly disestablished,"[25] that is, our own. Let me put it this way: while the visible/invisible distinction has functioned in an imprecise yet significant manner in historic Protestant and other contexts, its function

24. Hendrikus Berkhof, *Christian Faith: An Introduction to the Study of the Faith*, trans. Sierd Woudstra (Grand Rapids: Eerdmans, 1979), 398–99.

25. George A. Lindbeck, *The Nature of Doctrine: Religion and Theology in a Postliberal Age* (Philadelphia: Westminster, 1984), 134.

has been largely negative. That is to say, it has been concerned almost exclusively with the status of the institutional (visible) church. At its worst, it has served as a diatribe against Roman Catholic and other bodies perceived by nonconformists as boastful and presumptuous; at its best it has caused honest souls to check, within themselves, the all too human presumption of righteousness and finality. In other words, the distinction has been used mainly as a *critical* principle guarding against arrogance on the part of the visible church. Like John the Baptist, it has warned those who consider themselves Christians that "God is able from these very stones to raise up children to Abraham!"(Luke 3:8, RSV). "Many whom the church has, God does not have"!

Keeping the church humble is indeed a worthy cause, and never irrelevant. It belongs to the prophetic traditions of Scripture and is at the heart of what Paul Tillich called the Protestant principle. To insist, over against the prideful, exclusivistic *presumption* of secure belonging that the true church is visible only to God, is to insist with equal vigor that the *visible* church is always an admixture of things (*corpus permixtum*), whose authenticity and integrity can never be taken for granted. "Let him who stands take heed lest he fall" (1 Corinthians 10:12, RSV)! But while this critical aspect of the visible/invisible concept has exercised a certain influence in Protestantism, the constructive or affirmative dimension of the distinction has not, in my opinion.

To grasp the constructive aspect of this teaching, one must shift one's attention from the visible to the invisible side of the couplet. While the negative aspect insists that the true church cannot be equated with the visible church, the positive side asks whether the invisible church—i.e., the one known only to God—may not be found also outside the boundaries of the visible church. (Remember, says Augustine, "*Many whom God has, the church does not have*"!) To ask this earnestly, Christians must not only *ask* it; they must *act* as though such a thing might be entirely and quite concretely so. The church that takes seriously the prospect that authentic faith may well exist beyond the pale continuously *opens itself* to the world, expecting to find there instances of a faith that it can recognize as compatible with its own—and perhaps even more genuine than its own!

At very least, Scripture warns us, the church should not be surprised by such instances! An incident in the earliest of the four Gospels (Mark 9:38–39) is especially instructive in this regard. The disciples of Jesus had discovered someone "casting out demons" in Jesus's name. They were deeply offended, and attempted to stop this imposter from his illegitimate exorcism. In language all too characteristic of the centuries-old religious mentality that guards the gates, the disciples explain, "He was not following *us!*" (N.B.: not you but us!).

Jesus's response is permanently relevant: "'Whoever is not against us is for us.'" —

> "for no one who does a deed of power in my name will be able soon afterward to speak evil of me . . . For truly I tell you, whoever gives you a cup of water to drink because you bear the name of Christ will by no means lose the reward." (NRSV)

An even more pointed warning against ecclesiastical presumption is found in the New Testament's account of Jesus's encounter with an officer of the hated Roman occupiers. This man, a centurian, had approached Jesus with an urgent appeal: his servant (not a relative but an ordinary slave!) was paralyzed and "in distress" in the officer's home. The appellant was not so bold as to ask Jesus to come with him but told him, "only speak the word and my servant will be healed. For I am also a man under authority, with soldiers under me; and I say t one 'Go,' and he goes, and to another 'Come,' and he comes, and to my slave 'Do this,' and the slave does it.

> *When he heard this Jesus was amazed,* and said to those who followed him, "Truly I tell you, in no one in Israel have I found such faith. I tell you, many will come from east and west and will eat with Abraham and Jacob in the kingdom of heaven, while the heirs of the kingdom will be thrown into outer darkness, where there will be weeping and gnashing of teeth."
> And to the centurian Jesus said, "Go, let it be done for you according to your faith." And the servant was healed in that hour. (Matthew 8:5–13, NRSV)

Exegetes have attributed this and similar Matthean passages to the author's anti-Jewish bias, and throughout the ages Christians have been more than willing to follow suit, using this and other New Testament texts to demonstrate that the people of the "old covenant" had been supplanted (superseded) by the people of the "new covenant." But if the contemporary church cannot hear in such Scriptures a message precisely intended for itself , it will not only have lost touch with the prophetic thrust of the entire tradition of Jerusalem, it will also have repressed the hard twentieth-century lessons of Christian anti-Judaism; for, as Rosemary Radford Ruether and others have shown, the Holocaust of the Jews is inseparable from just this supersessionism.[26] Today, however, when the triumphalism of our once-imperial religion is being chastened on every side by the realities of secularism and religious pluralism, it is not so important that we should hear, in this fascinating text, the judgment of the presumptuous as it is that we should ponder Jesus's recognition of the faith of this despised outsider, and learn to detect in Jesus's "amazed" response to the centurian a timely lesson for our own mission. "Many whom God has, the church does not have."

ANONYMOUS CHRISTIANITY[·]

In some ways post–Vatican II Roman Catholicism has surpassed contemporary Protestantism in its openness to the reality that Augustine signaled when he wrote those words. While the Second Vatican Council certainly did not repudiate the *Extra ecclesiam nulla salus* dogma, and while in the decades after the Council conservative powers in Rome have made great strides in recovering the *narrower* applications of that dogma, the Council itself was sufficiently moved by its more imaginative participants to explore alternatives to the exclusivity of the Roman Catholic past. Among these insightful persons, none was more articulate and influential than the late Karl Rahner, perhaps the most important Catholic theologian of the twentieth century. Rahner wrote:

> If once we have the courage to give up our defence of the old facades which have nothing or very little behind them; if we cease to maintain, in public, the pretence of a universal Christendom; if we stop straining every nerve to get *everybody* baptized, to get *everybody* married in church and onto our registers (even when success means only, at bottom a victory for tradition, custom and ancestry, not for true faith and interior conviction); if, by letting all this go, we visibly relieve Christianity of the burdensome impression that it accepts responsibility for everything that goes on under this Christian top-dressing, the impression that Christianity is *natura sua* a sort of Everyman's Religious Varnish, a folk-religion (at the same level as that of folk-costumes)—then we can be free for real missionary adventures and apostolic self-confidence. Then we should not need to sigh and say, "We *still* have 15 per cent"; we could say "We're up to 17 per cent already". Just where is it written that *we* must have the whole 100 per cent? God must have

---

26. See Rosemary Radford Ruether, *Faith and Fratricide: The Theological Roots of Anti-Seminitism* (New York: Seabury, 1974)

all. We hope that he takes pity on all and will have all indeed. But we cannot say that he is doing so only if we, meaning the Church, have everybody.

Why should we not today alter to our use, quite humbly and dispassionately, a saying of St. Augustine's: Many whom God has, the Church does not have; and many whom the Church has God does not have? Why, in our defeatism, which springs from a muddled feeling of pity for mankind, do we forget that it is not truth but a heresy that there is no grace outside the Church? If we would only rid ourselves of these prejudices, grafted into us by the external Christianity of the West, we should not then feel inclined to engage in combat only if we immediately won a 100 per cent victory; we should then be justifiably proud and thankful if we won just one new Christian, instead of burying our ostrich-heads in the shifting sands of those who are Christians already.[27]

There is a boldness in these lines of the great German Catholic lacking in most Protestant (as well as *most* authoritative Catholic and Orthodox) ecclesiology; in fact mainstream Protestants, reading this passage *attentively,* would surely be shocked by it. What makes Rahner's thought all the more provocative is that unlike some of his more liberal Catholic contemporaries (Hans Küng, for example), he is not proposing that what he called "anonymous Christianity" should *replace* or *displace* the seriousness with which the *visible* church should be taken. Like Calvin and the other major Reformers, he insisted that honor be paid to the Christianity that names itself such. But Rahner obviously felt, not only that Christians ought to be more conscious of the grace of God at work in *the world*, but that they should pay *less* attention to the maintenance of the church and its precious boundaries.

That, I believe, is a judgement applicable to all the churches, including the *dispirited remnants of Protestant Establishment,*[28] which still pine inwardly for their reputedly glorious past, or seek in vain to retrieve it, or succumb fatalistically to their reduced and humiliated estate. So much of the energy—the planning, the recruitment of personnel, the interminable rearrangement of ecclesiastical structures, the building programs and

27. Karl Rahner, *Mission and Grace: Essays in Pastoral Theology*, vol. 1, trans. Cecily Hastings (London: Sheed & Ward, 1963), 50–51 (italics added).

28. See Hall, *Waiting for Gospel: An Appeal to the Dispirited Remnants of Protestant "Establishment"* (Eugene, OR: Cascade Books, 2012).

upkeep, the insistent scramble for money mistakenly called stewardship, and the marketing (mainline Protestantism's current substitution for evangelism!)—*so much* of the energy, ingenuity, and expectancy of the churches has been expended on *the church itself* that anyone assessing the situation objectively would have to conclude that the church is indeed, for Christians, the end of the matter and not only a means to some greater end. In short, the message that we have been rallying around and sending out into the world, the newfound worldliness of some of us notwithstanding, is that *Christianity is the Church.*

To state the matter differently, the *institutional* is still triumphing over the *organic* conception of the body of Christ; *religion* is still triumphing over *faith*. As noted heretofore, theologians from Barth and Tillich to Moltmann have been saying that Jesus Christ did not appear on earth to create yet another religion; but religion is still what the church seems to be about. Dietrich Bonhoeffer, in his later writings, charged that Christianity as represented by the church, is so thoroughly "soaked in religious consciousness," so completely defined by religion and not by faith, that it would be years before Christianity could be sufficiently liberated from religion to permit untrammeled reflection on *what Christianity really is*. Since Bonhoeffer—nearly seventy years ago!—threw out his challenge to serious Christians to develop and work for a "religionless Christianity,"[29] many Christian scholars and thinkers have attempted to move the churches in that direction—or at least to alert them to the difference between religion and faith. But far too little change can be noticed. Thus, many of us have accentuated the *movement* quality of the church in its original conception; but church buildings, both old and new, quietly but effectively announce that permanence is the norm. As we have noticed here again, the apostolicity of the church implies a radical critique of the *settled* state; but no congregation is as agitated as one having to meet in school basements or people's houses: it cannot be satisfied until the new church has been put up. All the same, discipleship means following the one who said that "'foxes have holes, and the birds of the air have nests; but the Son of Man has nowhere to lay his head" (Luke 9:58, NRSV). Like ancient Israel, the movement begun by the Nazarene was conceived as a wandering people—a people that is most faithful when it is least secure: tents and not houses are its proper dwelling-place.[30] But, also like ancient Israel, the church seems fated to seek

29. Bonhoeffer, *Letters and Papers from Prison*, 121ff.

30. Read in this connection the sermon of Stephen in Acts 7. Sir George McLeod

permanence, stability, security. It is true that the centuries have witnessed critical reactions to this religious quest and preoccupation: the monastic movement acquired a good deal of support, following the Constantinian-Theodosian establishment, from men and women who were looking for something different from mere religion. Alas, monastic and other alternatives to religious establishment, including Protestant alternatives, regularly devolved into new expressions of religious establishment. Almost every time some preacher of reform tried to recall alternative movements to their original simplicity (baggage strictly limited for the journey!), the reform failed after a relatively short period. Sometimes, ironically, reform failed most spectacularly when its very simplicity and discipline made it successful in conspicuously worldly terms.

The story of Francis of Assisi and his Little Brothers is a case in point: the failure of a dream brought about by its worldly success! Yet the failure or compromise of the Franciscan vision does not invalidate the vision itself. One of the most canny and powerful popes in history, listening reluctantly to the vision of Francis, realized that this manner of vision could not be written off as an impossible and dangerous idealism. In point of fact, it may be that Innocent III (the pope in question) was induced to bless Francis's little enterprise for purely pragmatic reasons; yet at least one of his cardinals considered the thing more deeply.

> Cardinal San Paolo seems to have argued more or less in this manner: it may be a hard life, but after all it is the life apparently described as ideal in the Gospel; make what compromises you think wise or humane about that ideal; but do not commit yourselves to saying that men shall *not* fulfil that ideal if they can.[31]

What we need especially to notice in this still evocative story from the thirteenth century (it is not the only story of its kind, but it is perhaps the most dramatic) is the reason why the vision of Francis was so offensive to many. The real reason is not the one that was most spoken about. Superficially, what bothered Francis's critics was the extraordinary rigor of the mendicant life Francis proposed: how could ordinary human beings endure the demands of a life that required so much sacrifice and insecurity—hand-to-mouth living on a grand scale! But what was *truly* offensive to the Christian establishment of Francis's epoch, and more particularly to

---

of Iona used to say of it that it is the best sermon in the New Testament—and it was 'preached by a layman"!

31. G. K. Chesterton, *St. Francis of Assisi* (Garden City, NY: Image, 1957), 100.

the established (especially the powerful Benedictine) patterns of monasticism itself, was the fact that Francis and his followers had challenged the chief *organizational* principle of monasticism, namely, the commitment to permanence of place—*stabilitas loci*. Francis's Little Brothers gladly embraced the other requirements of the monastic life—poverty, chastity, and obedience. They took these requirements for granted. But they wanted to move about in the world, freely and without the encumbrance of properties and possessions. They would depend upon heaven and the kindness of strangers for their sustenance; they would be mendicants, beggars. That was their great offense. It was, to be sure, a daring thing. Who could live in this world without the security of home, regular if not sumptuous meals, decent if not fashionable dress, and so on? How could any body of Christians exist without a good deal of attention to organization? And how could organization, to serve the varied needs of the community, not become increasingly *micro*-oranization? And how could such bureaucratized management not lead to institutional forms and economic stress and the maintenance of property and a growing body of administrators? Thus does realism squelch—and usually in advance!—any dreams of difference and change. The status quo has a head start over innovation, and it nearly always overcomes. But its victory in Christian history is always, and shall always be, at the cost of dispensing with, suppressing and repressing the very *charter* of the Christian movement: "*Go. . . . !* "

What this apostolic charter demands is not in the first place a program of heroic asceticism or abysmal sacrifice. Sacrifice and suffering may come—probably will come, in some form, if those who hear the Great Commission are serious. But sacrifice and suffering are not what the disciple community seeks—a point that Bonhoeffer made with great effect in *The Cost of Discipleship*. What the disciple community seeks is to follow, to be obedient to the one who calls it to leave its nets and its preoccupations with self and move out into the world without having to know beforehand that all will be well. In short, to trust. Obedience to this command *may* involve homelessness and hunger and the renunciation of sex, as it did also for Francis; but these are only consequences, *for some,* of following the Christ; they are not of the essence, nor are they intended for all. What *is* mandatory for all who hear this call to discipleship is a transformation of *attitude and orientation.* In place of the mindset symbolized by the ancient monastic rule termed *stabilitas loci* (we may render it in today's folk speech as, Stay put! Don't move!), the community of the Way is called to risk venturing out into the

lpxyd understand.

world without the usual accoutrements of security. Does it mean getting rid of church properties that are no longer used to capacity?[32] Perhaps, in some cases. Perhaps not, in others. At very least it would mean refusing to be demoralized by the numerical failures of Christendom, the empty pews and grey heads, the loss of influence in high places. Innumerable problems confront churches if and when they gain insight into the impossibility of maintaining the status quo, and these problems will undoubtedly consume the attention of many ardent church folk for decades to come. But more important than any question of what is to be done with the vast material accumulations of Christendom is the question how, in its post-Christendom phase, the church ought to regard *the world*. For at least fifteen or sixteen centuries Western Christendom, wherever it has overcome its heaven-bent revulsion of this world, has seen the world as the object of its activism. Whether it expressed this activism in authoritarian, evangelical, or moralizing terms, the church's characteristic approach to its worldly context has been that of a purveyor of goods (information, ethical counsel, moral codes, spirituality) that, in its view, the world needed. So long as the world felt, or could be persuaded to feel, that it did indeed need these goods, the churches had a place in it; but with the diminishment of worldly demand, religious supply seems more and more superfluous.

How fundamentally it would change the (visible!) church were it to view the world, not as a field for its own variously conceived mission but as a sphere of grace in which God is already present and active! That, I sense, is what Karl Rahner was asking his church to do. It was certainly also Dietrich Bonhoeffer's appeal to the churches. The Christian, Bonhoeffer wrote,

> must plunge himself into the life of a godless world, without attempting to gloss over its ungodliness with a veneer of religion or trying to transfigure it. He must live a 'worldly' life and so participate in the suffering of God. He *may* live a worldly life as

32. In one of his least-known writings, *Outline for a Book*, Bonhoeffer proposed that the "consequences" of the "stocktaking of Christianity" that he hoped to develop in "a book not more than 100 pages long" would include a major housecleaning!

> "As a fresh start she [the Church] should give away all her endowments to the poor and needy. The clergy should live solely on the free-will offerings of their congregations, or possibly engage in some secular calling. She must take her part in the social life of the world, not lording it over men, but helping and serving them. She must tell men, whatever their calling, what it means to live in Christ, to exist for others. And in particular, our own Church will have to take a strong line with the blasphemies of *hybris*, power-worship, envy and humbug" (*Letters and Papers from Prison*, 180).

one emancipated from all false religions and obligations. To be a Christian does not mean to be religious in a particular way, to cultivate some particular form of asceticism . . . , but to be a man. It is not some religious act which makes a Christian what he is, but participation in the suffering of God in the life of the world.[33]

Bonhoeffer's American friend, the late theologian and ethicist Paul Lehmann, translated Bonhoeffer's inspirational exhortation into quite practical ethical language. Unfortunately, Lehmann's ethic—which was much more than an ethic!—did not achieve in North America the hearing that it deserved. Lehmann believed that Christians should regard the world, not in the first place as a sphere in which *they* were called to work, but as a sphere in which God is already at work "making and keeping human life human." The question that the church should always be asking, and seeking to answer *in and for that particular time and place* (context), is not, what should we do? but rather, where is God now at work in the world? What is *God* doing in this world, here and now, to make and to keep human life human? The extent to which the church discerns an answer or answers to *that* question will determine the nature and relevance of its own activity. Given such an orientation, the Christian community does not then enter the world as though the world were a place utterly discontinuous with itself but rather as a familiar sphere—familiar, not only as its own inevitable dwelling place, but for the more fundamental reason that the Creator/Redeemer God that it acknowledges is the very one whose Spirit moves mysteriously throughout the whole creation. In a real sense, the only difference between the church and the world is that the church, when it is attentive and faithful, knows something about the world that the world does not know about itself: *that it is greatly loved!*

> The difference between believers and unbelievers is not defined by church membership, or even, in the last analysis, by baptism. The difference is defined by imagination and behavioural sensitivity to what God is doing in the world to make and to keep human life human, to achieve the maturity of [humankind], that is, the new humanity.[34]

This approach to the nature and mission of the church is quite different from the liberal-activist approach, which conceives of the task of the church

33. Ibid., 166.

34. Paul Lehmann, *Ethics in a Christian Context* (New York: Harper & Row, 1963), 117.

as involving itself in the world with a view to changing the world—making it more just, more peaceful, more ecologically sensitive, more concerned for the marginalized, and so forth There is no quarrel here with such goals; the difference between the liberal-activist approach and that of Bonhoeffer and Lehmann (and others) is the difference between law and gospel. For the liberal-activist the Christian message is almost wholly in the imperative mood: Go and do thus and so. For Lehmann the ethical imperative, which can never be spelled out concretely in advance, is dependent upon the theological indicative: "*God is at work in the world making and keeping human life human.* If you really believe that, and if you are imaginatively attentive to the world in which the suffering God is at work, you will discern what your own task then and there ought to be." It is the difference between the ethics of principle (or ideology) and the ethics of discipleship.

But for our present discussion, the important point to notice is that church and world are not two separate spheres but a single theater of God's compassionate sovereignty—the sovereignty of the God who suffers with (*com-passio*) the whole, groaning creation. The invisible church is that unquantifiable, anonymous and boundaryless plenitude of those who, whatever they may be called, or whomsoever they may think they serve, are in fact living and acting, here and there, now and then, as (Lehmann's word) "mature" human beings, and therefore as persons who are imaging God.

In centuries past, the concept of the church invisible was employed chiefly to incorporate the multitude of Christians who lived in the past (including pagan philosophers like Plato and Aristotle) along with those who claimed Christian identity here and now. What is being suggested here is that without neglecting the past, the thought of the invisible church should concentrate on the present and future, so that those claiming membership in the visible church would be prepared to experience in their worldly context signs and intimations of a greater plenitude of persons and events in which their God is being imaged.

Only the most impoverished imagination could be led from such a thought to the notion that all such persons and eventualities were—if only hiddenly—simply Christian. No Muslim, Jewish, Buddhist, or Hindu believer; no avowedly secular, agnostic, or frankly atheistic person would find it salutary to be though a crypto-Christian! But that is not the point. The point is, rather, that *Christians*, contemplating the religiously pluralistic multiculture in which today they find themselves, should be given eyes and hearts able to discern the boundlessness of God's work in the world, and so to understand *themselves* as participants in a project (shall we call it God's kingdom?) that is infinitely greater than themselves and their own (diminishing) numbers! Just that is the posture and attitude one hears in a memorable and insightful statement of one of North America's most insightful Christian thinkers, H. Richard Niebuhr:

> I do not have the evidence which allows me to say that the miracle of faith in God is worked only by Jesus Christ and that it is never given to [human beings] outside the sphere of his working, though I may say that where I note its presence I posit the presence of something like Jesus Christ.[35]

"Many whom God has, the church does not have . . . ."

CONCLUSION: THE CHURCH AFTER CHRISTENDOM

Christianity, I have argued here, is not the church. That thesis, which is essential to the spirit of negative or apophatic theology guiding our thought in this study, is not merely negative in the usual sense. It will not have been fully understood, in fact, unless it is heard as a liberating thought. For surely in the current religious situation in the Western world, recognition that the future of Christianity is not dependent upon the future of our churches is a liberating thought for all who contemplate the journey ahead. It means that our hope for the future of *Christianity* is not predicated upon optimism concerning the future of the today's ecclesiastical organizations. So far as the churches are concerned, there is no reason to believe that their quantitative and qualitative diminishment, which has been underway for two or three centuries, will be greatly altered in the centuries ahead. Certainly the dream of a Christian world, a dream which for many reached its pinnacle in the nineteenth century with its slogan, "The Kingdom of God in Our Time," is one that Christians today neither *should* dream nor (realistically, responsibly) *could* dream. Given the religiously pluralistic (and volatile!) global situation, such a dream can only function at the level of sentiment and nostalgia, or, more dangerously as the ideological basis for a militant, distorted, and finally a pathetic bid for Christian hegemony. World-conquering Christianity was *always* a travesty of the disciple community depicted in the New Testament. It was *always* wrongheaded and an

---

35. H. Richard Niebuhr, "Reformation: The Continuing Imperative," *The Christian Century* 77 (1960) 249.

egregious misunderstanding of the Christian message and mission. Today, in addition to being ill conceived, it is irresponsible and absurd. From now on, Christians who are serious about their faith must dream quite different dreams. It seems probable that these different dreams, whatever they may be concretely, will all manifest a greater interest in the invisible church than has been the case throughout the Christendom centuries.

As for the churches—the *visible*, historical churches that we have known and still know—, they are in varying states of disarray. They have been thus for a very long time, even the most apparently successful of them. Ecclesiastical leadership, with few conspicuous exceptions, has been ignoring the diminishment and humiliation of the churches with what can only be considered a marvel of prolonged collective repression. Promoters of Christendom, especially in these times of open and silent hostility between world religions, point to the still seemingly impressive statistics of Christian belonging. We are told that there are more than two billion adherents to Christianity in the world (one-third of the planet's human population), compared with ("only") one-and-a-half billion Muslims, nine-hundred-thousand Hindus, and so on. But what these statistics do not and cannot tell us is manifold. They do not tell us (1) that the growth rate of Christianity has declined in thirty-five years (between 1970 and 2005) from 1.64 percent to 1.32 percent; (2) that the number of those throughout the world (but especially in formerly so-called Christian countries) who declare no religious affiliation at all accounts for 16 percent[36] of the global population, and is growing conspicuously; (3) that in the most developed parts of the world secular materialism is rampant and atheism increasingly outspoken; (4) that in the northern hemisphere generally (with the possible exception of the United States) Protestant and Catholic versions of Christianity alike have suffered conspicuous losses both of numbers and influence, and often are riddled by internal dissension, sexual and other scandals, and so forth; (5) above all, these statistics do not tell us what percentage of the alleged 2.1+ billion Christians in the world are actively engaged with the churches to which they claim adherence, or have more than a rudimentary or hearsay awareness of what this faith teaches, or are profoundly influenced by this faith in their political, economic, cultural, and ethical choices.

The truth is that Christianity in the West, where it has had in the past its most impressive triumphs, has been experiencing decline for several

---

36. That is to say more than all religions other than Christianity and Islam, and half the number of Christians.

centuries—some would say from the end of the Middle Ages, though most would extend Christendom so far as the beginnings of the modern epoch (the eigteenth century), with geographic variations, some of them marked. Moreover, the "end of the constantinian era" (as it has been called) is not to be understood solely in quantitative terms; in fact, in a way the quantities are not very helpful at all, because what really matters in religious faith of every kind (namely, the authenticity or sincerity of belief, the depth of understanding) cannot be measured. Those who have most diligently tried to understand the *metamorphosis* through which Christianity has been passing in the modern epoch have for that reason depended very little on statistics. Statistics can be and frequently are terribly misleading. Full churches, seemingly official public approval, and religious rhetoric on the part of politicians (such as one has it today in the Republican Party of the USA) do not tell us anything very significant about the state of Christianity except that, like all religions, it can serve sociopolitical purposes that have little or no relationship with the faith being professed. When Søren Kierkegaard (1813–1855) became the first major critic of Christendom in modern Europe, the churches in Denmark, including his own *Frukirche* in Copenhagen, were full: Everybody was Christian! Denmark was Christian! Europe was Christian! And it was precisely this powerful, populous Christendom that Kierkegaard attacked—in the name of Jesus Christ! The failure of Christendom is not its quantitative but its qualitative losses. It is not accidental that in all Western lands, including the United States of America, the social groupings most conspicuously absent from the churches are the intellectuals, the artists, university professors and students, and serious searchers after truth and direction in their lives. With exceptions (some of them notable), *thinking* persons—or those most equipped to think, and most driven to do so—are not found in our churches. It is not necessary to employ the language of dumbing down to recognize that most popular expressions of Christianity, at least in North America, offer little to stimulate or satisfy the inquiring mind, and in the case of its more dogmatic and fundamentalist expressions the thinking public is simply repulsed. Though the popular media today have made the departure of the intelligentsia from the churches more conspicuous, it is not a new phenomenon. Dorothy Sayers, in her wartime BBC series *The Man Born to Be King*, put her finger on the problem:

> Not Herod, not Caiaphas, not Pilate, not Judas ever contrived
> to fasten upon Jesus Christ the reproach of insipidity; that final

indignity was left for pious hands to inflict. To make of his story something that could neither startle, nor shock, nor terrify, nor excite, nor inspire a living soul is to crucify the Son of God afresh and put him to an open shame . . . Let me tell you, good Christian people, an honest writer would be ashamed to treat a nursery tale as you have treated the greatest drama in history.[37]

Let me be quite clear: *none* of this means, nor should it be contrived to mean, that the churches ought to be written off, demeaned, or abandoned. The ecclesiology of the Reformers still applies: while the visible church is always an admixture of things, it must be taken seriously and responsibly served by all Christians. Out of these dry bones, the remnants of once powerful Christendom, the Spirit of God may indeed make something: they may be part of the future that divine Providence is bringing to pass. But neither should our care, loyalty, and labor in behalf of these churches detract from the more expansive (and less visible!) mission of God in God's groaning creation. Christianity in the form that it has assumed in the West for a millennium and a half—the form of Christendom, of Catholicism, or Orthodoxy or Protestantism; the form of denominations and salaried clergy and head offices and building projects, and so on: this Christianity has been fading, will fade increasingly, and may fade altogether; but it does not mean that Christianity itself is heading toward extinction. A statement on the Christian future made by the Anglican seer F. W. Robertson before the middle of the nineteenth century[38] seems to me to point to the manner of future orientation appropriate to Christian thinking today:

As to our 'incomparable Church', why it does not require a prophetic spirit to see that in ten years more she must be in fragments, *out of which fragments God will construct something for which I am content to wait.*

A century later, Paul Tillich wrote something similar: "[the] new form of Christianity [cannot] be named yet, [though it is] to be expected and prepared for [and] elements of it can be described."[39]

---

37. Quoted by Paul Scherer in *For We Have This Treasure*; The Yale Lectures on Preaching (New York: Harper, 1944), 134.

38. And quoted by another Anglican theologian, Alec Vidler, in his *The Church in an Age of Revolution* (Middlesex, UK: Penguin, 1961), 239.

39. Paul Tillich, *The Protestant Era*, trans. James Luther Adams (Chicago: University of Chicago Press, 1948), xxii.

We are, I think, still waiting to see what form the Christianity of the future may take. The mills of God grind much more slowly than the present age of rapid social change has conditioned most of us to think. The great transitions in the history of the Christian movement have taken centuries, and most of them were transitions *within* Christendom. The present transition (I prefer to call it a metamorphosis) is occurring *after* Christendom and in the midst of a chaotic but profoundly connected globalism that is both religionless and extravagantly, dangerously religious! Karl Rahner's generalization about the present state of Christianity seems to me pertinent still:

> our present situation is one of a transition from church sustained by a homogeneously Christian society and almost identical with it, from a people's church, to a church made up of those who have struggled against their environment, in order to reach a personally clear and responsible decision of faith.[40]

What such an assessment of our situation suggests (I think rightly) is that the Christianity of the future will be far less structured and far more dependent on personal reflection and decision than the Christianity to which so many centuries have conditioned us to expect. Perhaps, if the growing churches of the southern hemisphere can overcome their temptation to imitate the triumphalism of Western Christendom, the new Christianity will be a product of their fresh encounter with the Scriptures. Perhaps, as Christians in the developed world encounter not only the militancy but also the sincerity and depth of other faith traditions, some will be moved to consider more deeply the uniqueness of their own faith, at whose center there is One who loves creation but also evokes in the *human* creature a new sense of its capacity for compassion and stewardship.

In any case, one suspects that the churches—the visible face of Christianity—will have to be subjected to greater humiliations than we have seen thus far, and that many will fall away. From the perspective of the grandeur we imagine Christianity once enjoyed, what lies ahead will likely seem pure failure and catastrophe—a veritable *Goetterdaemerung*, though not so dramatic and obvious as Wagner's version, because it will undoubtedly occur incrementally, as it has been happening now for two or three centuries.

But whatever, concretely, may prove to be the future of Christianity, those who are anchored in the biblical witness and in the great and lasting

---

40. Karl Rahner, *The Practice of Faith: A Handbook of Contemporary Spirituality* (New York: Crossroads, 1983), 33.

counsels of theological tradition will be sustained by the knowledge that, after all, Christianity is *not the church*, that "many whom the church has, God does not have," and (above all!) that "many whom God has, the church does not have."

6

Not "the Truth"

Pilate asked Jesus, 'What is truth?'
Jesus said, 'I am ... the truth.'[1]

THE TRUTH THAT POSSESSES *US*

IT SHOULD BE OBVIOUS to Christians why the question of truth has to be approached apophatically, for they know, or should know, that truth is a living thing and cannot be held down and dissected—or even adequately described. Besides, *we* are living things ourselves; so it is a case of people on the run trying to read a reality also perpetually in motion. As Reinhold Niebuhr wrote in his Gifford Lectures of 1939, in a chapter insightfully entitled "Having, and Not Having, the Truth": "We know that the freedom of the human spirit over the flux of nature and history makes it impossible to accept *our* truth as *the* truth."[2]

Perhaps, however, we can say what the truth is *not*; certainly, as Christians, we shall be constrained to admit that *we* do not and cannot *possess* the truth. If the Christ is the Truth, then *Christianity,* so long as it bears witness to *Him,* cannot be.

> No one, not even a believer or a church, can boast of possessing truth, just as no one can boast of possessing love.[3]

---

1. St John's Gospel, 18:38, and 14:6

2. *The Nature and Destiny of Man* (New York: Scribner, 1953), 2:214.

3. Paul Tillich, *On the Boundary: An Autobiographical Sketch* (New York: Scribner, 1966), 51.

As the juxtaposition of the two short sentences at the head of this chapter makes perfectly clear, the only *great* truth we know as Christians is *a truth that possesses us!* Occasionally, we are allowed to glimpse that truth, as though "through a glass, darkly." But we cannot *have* it.[4] For Christian faith there could be no greater demonstration of arrogance and error than claiming to have the Truth. What we glimpse of the living Truth is always limited by our own incapacity for receiving it—and also, not incidentally, by our hidden *aversion* to it! Let us not pretend that we are all just panting for the gospel of . . . the cross! Thus for many reasons, we know, when we are honest, that "*our* truth is not *the* truth." Even Moses was only allowed to see, *en passant*, the back parts of Yahweh (Exodus 33:23). If like Moses, we are enabled by divine forbearance now and then to sense, briefly, a Presence that overwhelms us with its Ultimacy, we may count ourselves among the favored of the earth—though where that leads may not be what we had in mind! With the Incarnation of the Word, we believe, Truth has come closer—Oh! has come and "lived among us" (cf. John 1:14). But that awesome proximity only heightens, for Christians, the tremendous mystery of God's Truth; for it reveals, at bottom, a judgment and a compassion (a compassion, yes—but also a judgement!) that utterly transcend both our imagination and our deserving. Confronted by that One, the One who *is the Truth*, we can only say, with St Peter, "Go away from me, Lord, for I am a sinful man" (Luke 5:8, NRSV).

"Having, and not having, the truth," we are thus no strangers to Pilate's question. "Jesting Pilate," wrote Coleridge in his book on truth, "would not stay for an answer." We Christians, intrigued by the little that we have glimpsed of the living truth, do, some of us, "stay for an answer," and like everyone else we would prefer to have that answer in straightforward, portable terms! So we construct theologies and christologies and pneumatologies out of our collective brief encounters with the Indescribable. This is allowed, despite the fact that it is, *mostly*, a childish attempt to tame the wild thing that will not be domesticated. It is only authentic, really, this theologizing of ours, when it leads us back, humbled, to the living Answer that is as much question as answer. That Answer is both the illumination and the enigma that colors our faith. And it is always some version of the answer Pilate did not wait for (though it had been uttered four chapters earlier than Pilate's question!): "I am . . . the truth" (*Ego sum via, veritas, et vita*).

4. See chapter 2 for my reference to Billy Graham's visit to Union Theological Seminary in the 1950s.

Was that the statement of an egoist, or of *another* "Jester"?—perhaps even a madman? Perhaps, in some Dostoevskyan sense. But no. For John, whose gospel account, as is well known, differs in both tone and content from the work of the other three evangelists, it is strictly consistent with his whole approach. "Your *word* is truth," says Jesus to his Father in John's account of what is commonly called Jesus's high-priestly prayer (17:17); and, as the beautiful Prologue of John's gospel insists, God's Word (*Logos*), which was *with* God and *was* God from the beginning, in Jesus had "become flesh" (1:14). Jesus *was*, for St. John, God's very *Logos*—the divine, living, creating, indefinable Word incarnate, and therefore the truth. *The Truth!*

A DIFFERENT WAY OF THINKING

But how could this be? What could possibly be meant by such a declaration?—*I am the truth!* If someone made a statement like this in our presence today—perhaps an acquaintance given to dramatic pronouncements—we would, most of us, be nonplussed, if not downright dismissive. Eyebrows would be raised, sly looks would be exchanged. In time, if such nonsensical utterances continued from that source, mention would be made of megalomania, and there would be whispered suggestions of the need for counseling, psychiatric help, and pharmaceuticals!

The fact is that here we have entered a thought-world almost totally unlike our own, or at least one that is so alien to the dominant manner of thinking in contemporary Western societies that in order to comprehend it even minimally, we shall have to embark upon a rather long and involved analysis. Perhaps, however, we shall find that this other thought-world can, if imaginatively presented, count on some distant echoes in our own subterranean consciousness, our greatly concealed and repressed and many-sided self. It will help, certainly, if we have been avid readers of novels or lovers of stories—including viewers of good films. For literature and the arts, so far as they are significant in our lives, can deliver us from complete captivation by the modern assumption that *truth* can be entertained only of realities that can be submitted to empirical verification. Perhaps there is still within us a sufficient sense of wonder to serve as a secret doorway into the hidden garden of John of Patmos, who saw truth, at its highest and deepest, in the being (the I-am-ness!) of a life, a *Person*.[5]

5. As Trinitarian theology reminds us, the word *person* ("One God in Three *Persons*")

At any rate, we shall have to attempt something like that pilgrimage to another thought-world if we wish to think *theologically*, in the Christian mode. The greatest handicap to such a journey—indeed to the whole vocation of *theology*—is the problem to which I have just alluded, namely, the ubiquity of the modern reduction of truth to matters scientifically verifiable—not just to reason (the indispensable dialogue partner and assessor of revealed truth in the medieval world) but to a particular and much-reduced and circumscribed *type* of reason that for the most part refuses any kind of interaction with revelation. So powerful and widespread is this epistemological/axiological assumption that even though at least 90 percent of human experience precludes subjection to empirical verification, everyone from every walk of life today pays silent if not outspoken homage to it. We reduce to opinion or poetry or feeling all human experience that eludes scientific investigation. We manifest an intuitive hesitancy, sometimes even shame, about claiming truth for anything that cannot be *proven* so. The tyranny of scientific method affects every aspect of our life. Human relationships—friendship, love, collegiality, and the like—which are by definition subjective and unquantifiable, are under an invisible strain in such a society, precisely because they defy certitude. Is it really true that my wife loves me, or that my friend is loyal to me, or that my colleagues respect me; how can I *know* that? Declarations of love, or friendship, or collegiality are only words. There may have been a time (the novels of the nineteenth century suggest there really was a time) when one's word was sufficient proof of true intent; those who did not keep their word dishonored both themselves and their civilization, class, or station. By comparison, our society today is a society of documentation, legalization, and therefore, by implication, of a ubiquitous and sustained suspicion. Every deed, not only those suspected of criminal intent, has its paper trail. If we cannot prove empirically that something in the realm of human relationships is true, then we must come as closely as possible to doing so; hard evidence is the next best thing to value-free testing and verification.

This commitment to empirical verifiability also affects religion—and in a manner that has become both tedious and exasperating for Christians who understand something of this other thought-world we are trying to comprehend just now. Since, quite obviously, matters of religious belief are *not* subjectable to empirical verification, large numbers of Christians who

---

is derived from ancient drama: one *sona* (sound/voice) emanates through (*per*) three different masks.

are, as contemporary men and women, psychically and intellectually beholden to this scientific Golden Rule of genuine knowledge and truth, are driven to inept *imitative* methods of verification. They claim (for example) objective, demonstrable truth for the Bible or for this or that dogmatic tradition. It is of course a naïve and pathetic imitation of natural science, but one cannot overstate, I think, the influence of the victory of the scientific mindset in the genesis of religious fundamentalism, whether biblicism or dogmatism. In a context where the idea of truth is so thoroughly conditioned by empiricism and pragmatism, the religious feel an almost palpable constraint to *imitate* empirical method even when by definition they cannot *duplicate* it. The religious imitation is inevitably unsophisticated, if not patently absurd; but it suffices, apparently, for large numbers of Christians on this continent who (for example) use Genesis as proof of the truth of their creationist beliefs in a manner not *entirely* remote from the popular evolutionist's use of Darwin. The conclusions are of course antithetical, but the methodologies are provocatively (though not convincingly) analogous.

Truth in the biblical sense, however—that is to say a sense quite different from biblicism!—assumes quite another point of departure. Biblical faith, whether that means the Bible itself or the traditions that have understood Scripture profoundly, is of course not *dis*interested in *facts* and the demonstration of their truth. Taking into account the evolution of historical method, it is remarkable how keen are the gospel writers, for example, to document the facticity of their testimonies to the movements, acts, and words of Jesus of Nazareth. Yet the primary and indispensable orientation of the scriptural authors does not lie in that direction. For the tradition of Jerusalem, truth is a category of *relationship* and of the *livingness*, that is, of the contextual concreteness and ongoingness, that characterize all relationships. This observation, however, requires a more explicit discussion before we can proceed.

RELATIONALITY AS THE FRAMEWORK OF BIBLICAL THOUGHT ABOUT TRUTH

It is not extraordinary to claim that truth, in biblical thought, is a *relational* concept; for in fact all the major categories of biblical thought are steeped in relationality and can only be misunderstood if they are divorced from that ontological background assumption. All!—not merely the more obviously relational categories like love, faith, and hope; compassion; justice;

goodness; and the like; i.e., categories that all possess primary *verbal* meanings and require objects, but also those categories that appear, at first, simply *nouns*. Consider the two most central of these latter: God and Man (*der Mensch* [humans, humankind]).

(i) We do not hear of the Deity in the Hebrew and Christian Scriptures, apart from God's acting—and acting, normally, in relation to created beings, especially humans. There is no abstract discussion of *Yahweh/Theos* in the Bible, such as one has in Aristotle and other classical philosophers. From the beginning God is a doing, relating, responding, and notably a *speaking* God: *Deus loquens*. A God whose *Word* is truth (John 17). The whole story told in the continuity of the older and newer Testaments is centered in God's *engagement* of the creature, especially the human creature, who is the created dialogue partner of the Creator: *Homo loquens*. "'Adam, where art thou?'" (Genesis 3:9, KJV) could be the title of the entire story told in these pages, and in that case the *subtitle* would have to be, "I heard the sound of thee, and I was afraid because I was naked" (3:10). God is never God in Holy Isolation—never "One is one, and all alone, and evermore shall be so."[6] Truly, God is Other—even, in Rudolf Otto's expression, *wholly Other, totaliter aliter*. But, precisely as this *Other*, God seeks and confronts (Francis Thompson would say *hounds!*) humankind. The biblical God is God in relationship: the "Eternal Thou" (Buber) who searches for and addresses the human I and We.

Beyond that, we must note that even *in Godself*, so far as biblical thought allows such a thought, there seems to be dialogue, relatedness. The monotheism of the tradition of Jerusalem is not an ideological commitment to the number 1. Such a commitment does seems to be characteristic of Islamic and some other religious and philosophic forms of monotheism, but for the tradition of Jerusalem, in both its Jewish and its Christian forms, there is dialogue *within* the deity, even at the risk of courting a certain dualism (or, in the case of Christian theology, tritheism). This is seen, for example, in one of the names by which early Judaism knew God: *Elohim*, a plural term, which literally rendered would have to be translated as 'Gods', or perhaps 'the Godhead'. God, in the Hebrew scriptures, is often depicted

---

6. From "Green Grow the Rushes, O." This traditional English song, the roots of which are difficult to trace, seems to refer in its opening verse to the One God. But as some commentators have noted, the Trinitarian conception of God that dominated the spirituality of ancient Christian England would not have supported such a Unitarian kind of monotheism, which, they note, is closer to Muslim than to Christian conceptions of the deity.

as being in dialogue with himself, weighing different possibilities, allowing his mercy to temper his wrath, trying to understand, trying to decide![7]

Therefore Jesus, the incarnation of the divine *Logos*, is frequently seen in rapt *discussion* or even *argumentation* (prayer!) with his Father; and in view of the apparent incapacity of humans to comprehend the truth that he represents, the truth that he *is*, Jesus promises to send "another counselor" "the Spirit of Truth," who will "lead you into all truth" (John 14–15). It could be argued that both the incarnation and Trinity doctrines of Christianity grew out of the inexorable, innate longing of the Hebrew God to communicate his truth, that is to say, *himself*, to the strange, perhaps impossible but beloved creature *Adam* (the made-of-dust human). Jews, traditionally, have understood both the incarnation and the doctrine of the Trinity as violations of Hebraic monotheism; but it is the dialogical character of precisely *that* monotheism—mystical or dialectical monotheism, as Tillich has called it[8]—that provided Christians with the intellectual and spiritual background expressed in both the incarnation and the Trinity doctrines of Christian faith.[9]

What is being presupposed here is that the most rudimentary of all philosophic concepts, *ontology* or the theory of *being* (Aristotle calls it the 'first science,' *metaphysics*) is relational. As I have expressed it elsewhere,[10] in contrast to the tradition of Athens, the tradition of Jerusalem understands *being* to mean *being-with, Mitsein* (with-being). This foundational or rudimentary understanding of the nature of all that *is* quite naturally qualifies and colors every aspect of reality. A thing, a moment in time, above all a living being—all, everything, everyone: defined by their relatedness to others, to the interconnected whole. When, today, Christians use such terms

7. This sense of the deity's responsiveness and of human freedom and unpredictability is what informs process theology. The Creator too is as it were learning as He goes along.

8. "Trinitarian monotheism is not a matter of the number three. It is a qualitative and not a quantitative characterization of God. *It is an attempt to speak of the* living *God, the God in whom the ultimate and the concrete are united.*" Paul Tillich, *Systematic Theology* (Chicago: University of Chicago Press, 1951), 1:228; italics added.

9. The essentially *Hebraic* background of both Trinitarian and Christological theology has been obscured (for both Jewish and Christian communities) by the *language* that the theologians of the early church used to explicate them. That language, and much too frequently the conceptualization behind it, was decidedly *not* Hebraic; it was Greek and Hellenistic. But of course Judaism itself was significantly captivated by Hellenism.

10. See my *Thinking the Faith: Christian Theology in a North American Context* (Minneapolis: Augsburg, 1989), 288, 359–60, 382.

as *holistic* and *contextual*, this biblical ontology of communion (as I have sometimes named it) is the underlying *metaphysic* implied. (If this sounds a little like some of the musings of contemporary ecologists, it is only because ecology—whose genesis is inseparable from the enormous problems that arise when science [*scientia*] is reduced to verifiable data and thus to specializaation!—has had to explore the interconnectedness of things that biblical faith has known all along, even though the Christian defenders of the Bible rarely grasped this.)

(ii) Man—*homo sapiens*—the human being, also clearly a noun, has nevertheless an inherently *verbal* quality in biblical thought: this strange speaking animal is a being-towards and a being-with. "It is not good that the man should be alone," observed the Creator, learning as he went about his work (!). Human being is innately discontented with being alone, for the human (like all the other creatures according to their natures, but more intensely than most because of its vulnerability) is a form of being that is in itself directed towards the other. Human sexuality is only one dimension, though a conspicuous one, of this unavoidable other-directedness. For biblical faith, the other towards whom human being is directed is threefold: its Creator, its own kind (the woman, the man; the neighbor), and otherkind. The primal or foundational Other is the searching and speaking Source, the Creator-God. Augustine understood this well (better than monastics like Anselm and Aquinas) probably because he was a lover before he was a monk(!), and so it is not surprising that Augustine's most memorable sentence bespeaks both the divine Searcher ("Adam, where art thou?) and the hidden, frightened creature ("I was afraid, because I was naked"): *Tu fecisti nos ad te, Domine, et inquietum est cor nostrum donec requiescat in te!*[11]

This last-made and highly experimental (!) creature, the human, is said (Genesis 1:26–27) to be made in the image of God (*imago Dei*), and an erroneous but powerful and sticky interpretation of this term, taken together with an equally erroneous and equally powerful and sustained interpretation of another term or two in this same Priestly story of creation,[12] has caused Western Christendom and the successive cultures

11. Augustine, *Confessions,* book 1, paragraph 1: "Thou madest us for Thyself, and our heart is restless, until it repose in Thee." Edward B. Pusey, trans. *The Confessions of Saint Augustine* (New York: Modern Library, 1949), 3.

12. I refer of course to Genesis 1:28, where the Lord God commands the human pair to "multiply," "subdue," and "have dominion over" all the other species. Both the *imago Dei* and the concept of human "dominion", having been plucked out of the Bible and made to serve the anthropological ambitions of imperial peoples from ancient Athens

that it spawned to posit the noxious notion of *human* being as something entirely different from, and of course *higher* than, all other creaturely being. The erroneous character of the exegesis of these (and similar) texts must be traced precisely to the neglect, rejection, and almost total loss of the afore-mentioned relational ontology of biblical thought. The *imago Dei* is *not* a quality inhering in human being (e.g., rationality, volition) but the inher-ent and destined *orientation* of the human towards its Creator. As Calvin, rarely among Christian thinkers, understood, *like a mirror* we *image* (N. B. a verb) God *if and when and as we are turned toward God.* Our created nature, as Augustine realized, is indeed to be turned toward God, but our fallen nature is to be turned away from God and thus to *image* that, alas, to which we *are* turned—which is invariably a fallacious and pathetic object of "ultimate concern," as Tillich would say.

Human being therefore is prominent in biblical thought, not because the human is more precious to God or has the highest value on some fanci-ful hierarchy of being, but only because in the great (ecological!) scheme of things, this particular creature, the *speaking* creature, has been given a specific and unique *vocation*. It is a *representational*—if you like, a *priestly*, and certainly a *stewardly*—vocation; and for its actualization this vocation depends upon the human realization, not that it is separate from and high-er than other creatures but to the contrary that it is one with all the others. It can only speak (act) for the others when it knows itself to be entirely at one *with* the others! Its representative *vocation*, and therefore the gifts necessary to that vocation (reason, will, manual dexterity, and so forth) are entirely subordinate to the *primary* requirement of this vocation, which is (to state the matter in the most direct way) *to love.* And that primary requirement, which directs and qualifies all the other significant features of this creature's uniqueness (thinking, knowing, remembering, foreseeing, hoping, articulating) is, as C. F. von Weizsaecker has so eloquently said, precisely what is missing in the modern *imago hominis*: "The scientific and technical world of modern man is the result of his daring enterprise: *knowl-edge without love.*"[13]

---

and Rome to modern Europe and America, *badly require a critique and reorientation that puts them back into the* <u>relational ontology</u> of the tradition of Jerusalem! I have made a stab at this task in various publications, but notably in *Imaging God: Dominion as Stewardship* (1986; reprinted, Eugene, OR: Wipf & Stock, 2004).

13. C. F. Weizsaecker, *The History of Nature*, trans. Fred. D. Wieck (Chicago: Univer-sity of Chicago Press, 1949), 190 (italics added).

If, then, we have sufficiently sketched the ontological background, namely the biblical ontology of communion or *with-being*, we may return to the question at hand: how does such an ontology affect and condition the Christian understanding of the nature of *truth?*

TRUTH, RELATIONALLY CONCEIVED

As intimated, the relational ontology of the tradition of Jerusalem, expressed in its most rudimentary and concrete manner is simply, profoundly, the language of *love*: divine love (*agape*), love between human persons, and the love of creation. The Bible does not speak of ontology but of love. Love *is* the ontology of Holy Scripture. No other language can replace it. If in the foregoing we have employed metaphysical language of Athens, it is only to distinguish the biblical conception of what it means to be (i.e., to-be-*with*) from substantialistic and hierarchic conceptions of being. When the Bible declares that "God *is* love"; and when Jesus summarizes the entire thrust of the law and the prophets in two commandments (to love God and the neighbor), it is to be understood that they are drawing upon this rudimentary ontology of their whole tradition.

Given that foundation, *truth*, at its most basic, has to be understood as a component or quality of love. Thus Scripture regularly expresses the *truth of God* as God's steadfast love, God's *faithfulness*.

> In the O.T. truth is a quality which properly belongs to God. God is a God of truth (Ps. 31:5, Jeremiah 10:10) who 'keepeth truth forever' (Ps. 146:6, cf. 100:5). Truth means essentially reliability, dependableness, ability to perform what is required. The Hebrew words translated as.'truth' (*emeth, emunah*) are sometimes rendered 'faithfulness (Hosea 2:20, Deuteronomy 32:4 . . . cf. also Isaiah 25:1). The verb *aman* is more common than the nouns, and it means 'confirm,' 'stand firm,' 'trust'.[14]

The truth that the loving God requires of the beloved human is thus an "existential"[15] truth, which is to say a truth of "the inward parts" (Psalm 51:6), a truth which both reflects and enacts the divine love that is its

---

14. Alan Richardson, ed., *A Theological Word Book of the Bible* (London: SCM, 1950), 269.

15. "Religious truth is existential truth." Hendrikus Berkhof, *Christian Faith: An Introduction to the Study of the Faith*, trans. Sierd Woudstra (Grand Rapids: Eerdmans, 1979), 18.

genesis. It is not an abstract truth, divorced or divorceable from the actual living of life, but a truth that both talks the talk (Psalm 15:2) and walks the walk. (Second Kings 20:3 [RSV] actually anticipates that contemporary cliché when it has King Hezekiah pray thus: "Remember now, O Lord, I beseech thee, how I have walked before thee in faithfulness and with a whole heart, and have done what is good in thy sight.") Truth is something to be "walked in", not merely assented to. "If you believe these things," says Jesus to his listeners, "blessed are you if you *do* them" (John 13:17). Truth is at the same time rooted in faith (trust) and something to be done—at the same time a theological and an ethical concept.

This applies as much to the human-to-human relationship as to the divine-human relationship. What is required of all human love, whether it is directed toward the Creator or the fellow creature, is trust and faithfulness. As I reflect on this subject, my mind turns again and again to the ancient language of the Christian marriage service: "And thereto I plight thee my troth." *Troth* (Old English for "truth") contains both the idea of truthfulness and faithfulness or loyalty. To "plight" or pledge one's "troth" thus means to give the other one's truth, or (to express it differently but synonymously) to promise faithfulness toward the other. Here the *verbal*, active character of truth is articulated in the most concrete way. What the husband and wife promise one another is not simply always to tell the truth—to have no secrets, to share everything (as so much pseudoromantic parlance would have it), but rather to live and to do the truth in relation to this other—which is only to say, in different words, to *love* the other, really to be *with* and *for* the other; to manifest in relation to the other a *with-being* (*Mitsein*) that is at the same time a *with-suffering* (compassion; *Mitleid*). And this ontology of communion applies in all human dealings vis a vis the other, not only the other *human* but the other non- or extrahuman creature, whom the speaking creature (*Homo loquens*) represents.

When the interconnectedness of all that *is*, is thus the presupposition of the language of truth, truth cannot be reduced to data, fact, object. At its most foundational, truth understood within the ontology of relationality, which is to say (biblically) in the language of love, defies objectification and codification. Many *aspects* or manifestations of the truth may, and undoubtedly should, be subjected to tests of authenticity and critical analysis; but the underlying truth of relationships is existential—that is, a matter of living, remembering, hoping, suffering, longing, forgiving, beginning again, and countering the abysmal loneliness and alienation of the individual.

To make such claims for the *foundational* truth to which we are beckoned by the faithful and gracious Source of life does *not* mean that the ordinary, daily quest for *verity*—for truths—is neglected or despised by this tradition. *Of course* truth also means seeking, in one's daily acts and speech, genuine *correspondence* between reality and one's perceptions and valuations of reality. When the Jewish authors of the New Testament spoke of truth in the common language of their Mediterranean world, Greek, they used the word *aletheia*; and like so many Greek words, this word brought with it an ontological and theological worldview subtly different from the Hebrew words for "truth." That Hellenic and Hellenistic worldview, and the truth language that it contained, brought the newer Testamental conceptions of truth (as E. C. Blackman notes[16]) "nearer to our modern ones." But, as Blackman cautions, it must not be overlooked that the Jewish writers were *using* the language at hand (including *aletheia*) to express thoughts that were not the same, or not quite the same, as the thoughts in their minds as they wrote. Behind the Greek words lay Hebraic thoughts. While *aletheia* does, therefore, in some sense baptize the Platonic concern for clear thinking and the banishment of ignorance, and the Aristotelian concern for honest, empirically based perception, we need to hear behind this language the Hebraic insistence that truth is steeped both in the relational and the ethical: that is, it occurs within the framework of trusting relationships, and it issues in *deeds* of truth (John 3:21; 1 John 1:6):

> If we say that we have fellowship with him [God] while we walk in darkness, we lie and do not live according to the truth; but if we walk in the light, as he is in the light, we have fellowship with one another . . . (1 John 1:6–7, RSV)

The relational ontology applied to the definition of truth, which these sentences accurately reflect, by no means annuls or displaces the ordinary insistence that truths should conform to the realities to which they point. There is no quarrel here with science or even with empirical method—so long as it does not seek to become ultimate and absolute. But the chief concern of biblical faith is to preserve the veracity of the ultimate truth, which is the truth in which we "live and move and have our being," and therefore to preserve both its mystery and the modesty that is required of all who are turned towards it. But the expression "turned towards" leads us

---

16. Richardson, ed., *A Theological Word Book of the Bible*, 270.

immediately to our final and necessary observation about truth biblically conceived.

TRUTH-ORIENTATION

As we have seen with words like *Mitsein*, *Mitleid*, and others, the German language lends itself in many ways to the articulation of theological concepts that escape us in the Anglo-Saxon world, partly because our language has been so profoundly affected by Latin (making words like *being* and *compassion* almost technical for us), and partly because our philosophic preferences have been for empirical and pragmatic thought. For greater accuracy in the discussion of truth biblically conceived, we will draw now on another German word, a compound word that while it is not part of ordinary German discourse, is readily understood by readers of German and can convey to all of us an extremely important nuance—one that suggests a particularly significant directive thought about the nature of truth and our human relation to truth. I first learned this word in conversation with the great German physicist and lay theologian Carl-Friedrich von Weizsaecker. Professor Weizsaecker spoke of *Wahrheitsorientierung*: orientation (*orientierung*) towards truth (*Wahrheit*).

As we have seen in the previous discussion, Truth for Christians is a living, existential reality, most fully and ultimately expressed in the being, the complete *with-being* (solidarity) of the One who said, *Ego sum via, veritas, et vita* ("I am the way, the truth, and the life"). We, therefore, who believe we are the recipients of revealed Truth, know that we cannot *possess* the Truth that we, by faith, hear and (to some small extent) see. Precisely the revelation of this capital-*T* Truth prevents us from any kind of claim to *having* truth, and requires of us the greatest modesty in all our attempts to bear witness to the Truth we have met. Just this is what drove Luther to say that the revealing God (*Deus revelatus*) is at the same time—*in that very revealinig!*—*Deus absconditus*, the hidden God. God hides Godself in God's self-revelation.

This paradox sounds like a contradiction to all logical reasoners; yet it is neither unreasonable nor contradictory of ordinary, lived human experience. Who among all one's acquaintances remains the least known, the most hidden? Surely it is those—the one or two, the four or five—whom we know (in the usual sense) best! The mystery and hiddenness of their persons, their very being, is in fact the *conditio sine que non* of the uniqueness and depth of one's relationship with them. They have revealed enough of themselves to us to make us realize that we can never have them—that our images of them are always in some sense graven images, which must again and again be smashed in order that they, these others in all their specificity, can remain the persons they are to us: their *thou* must not be violated by definitions of them—must not be turned into *it* objects, whom we can manipulate and dominate and dismiss. As soon as we have exchanged the reality of their living persons into data (truths) on the basis of which we think we (finally!) truly understand them—as soon as this happens—we have in fact dismissed these others from any independent role in our lives and rendered them objects that no longer intrigue and fascinate and (yes!) threaten our own self-conceptions. The essential unknownness of the known, the *best*-known, is the very guarantor of our trust in, faithfulness towards, and love for them.[17]

So we cannot *have* the truth. We know, as Niebuhr says,[18] that "*our truth is not the truth.*" How could we imagine that we, who cannot even know *ourselves* fully or rightly, can know the other? As we cannot *understand* but only *stand under* the Truth that Jesus Christ is, neither, analogously, can we understand the *human* beloved, but can only stand under and live-with this other, being grateful for him/her/them, and responding in love to the love they show us. And this applies *mutatis mutandis* to our relationships with the other that is extrahuman, indeed to the other that is the living planet (as James Lovelock insists).[19]

Of course we experience this hiddenness of the revealed in deeply frustrating ways. We seek, often we *demand*, finality of understanding, certitude, closure! And this demand threatens to destroy all our relationships, because it asks for that which cannot be given—which, if it were given, would end the relationship! Our very *faith*, our *trust*, drives us to understand *now* and *completely*. *Fides quaerens intellectum!* Faith, in Anselm's phrase, must mean both trust in and struggle with God. (Remember, the name *Israel* means "the one who struggles with God.")

We cannot possess truth. That is the immovable limit within which, as humans and Christians, we stand. *But we <u>can be oriented toward Truth</u>.* We can be focused upon, ultimately concerned for, turned towards Truth. And, as the *imago Dei* concept insists, when our fallen creaturely orientation is

17. See in this connection the afterword.

18. See note 2 above.

19. See introduction, note 5, xxvii–xxviii.

righted and we are, in some measure, turned by the divine Spirit towards God and therefore, when we in some measure, mirror God, we are turned also and simultaneously towards Truth, for God's word *is* Truth. It is indeed all a matter of *orientation*. We humans are such creatures as are always turned towards something else, and this may mean, in the best case scenario, that we are so turned because we recognize the insufficiency of our selves; but it can also (and regularly does) mean that we are turned towards unworthy objects and objectives out of a fearful sense of insecurity ready to find security, acceptance, and finality in whatever seems—to our distorted understanding—to offer such assurances, and as quickly as possible! The history of humankind, and the biographies of all human persons living and dead, are variations on the theme of our incessant, fevered, and mostly pathetic turning. We turn madly from one false god to another, one ideology to another, one fashionable cause to another, one worldview to another, one alleged truth to another. In our aboriginal restlessness (Augustine), we flee continuously from the One in whom we could find rest—the one Truth that in denying us *securitas* offers us compassion and faithfulness. The story told in the continuity of the biblical Testaments is the story, first and foremost, of that One, who does not wait for us to turn to him, but who turns in greatest humility towards *us*, and through suffering and persistent love turns *us*, now and then, here and there, towards him—in acts of sheer grace termed in Scripture *metanoia*: repentance, rebirth; that is, a sheer turnaround!

We cannot *have* the Truth. *Christianity* does not *have* the Truth. The only thing that can be asked of Christianity, as of any other religion, ideology, or way or life, is whether it is oriented toward the Truth. And the very first test of whether such an orientation is really present is the extent to which the religion in question *knows and admits openly that it does not have, and is not, the Truth!* That is to say, *modesty* in respect to Truth is the earmark of authenticity.

And the second test of such an orientation is the presence in such a community of a certain critical vigilance about all exaggerated claims to final truth. If this tradition of Jerusalem is inherently nonideological, that is because it knows in its bones that ideology is always reductionistic, and especially that it reduces humans both individually and collectively, robbing them of their mystery as those who image a Truth beyond themselves.

But the third test of such an orientation is the sense of *gratitude* in such a community for all quests for truth and all contributions to the treasury of knowledge that emanate from modest sources that in their own ways and according to their own lights are also oriented toward truth. Christians know, and love, all who are oriented toward a truth they know they cannot know—whether they call that truth God or Life or the Absolute or *Gaia* or simply the Unknown; for these are likely to manifest a rudimentary sense of mystery and modesty also in relation to the truths that they do and can know. In the presence of their great truth, whatever it is, they are unlikely to elevate their smaller truths—their knowledge, their data, their carefully tested hypotheses—to the rank of the Absolute. Their scientific and historical and anthropological and sociological and economic and other truths are received with gratitude by Christians and by all genuine seekers after truth, because they betoken a human modesty that knows that it does not know—a virtue, not only for the tradition of Jerusalem but for at least that Platonic and Socratic dimension of the tradition of Athens which insists that the truly wise one is the one who knows that he is not wise.

Conclusion

The Face in the Space at the Center

> The face itself was concave, worn down with the constant treading. It was this concave face that had looked at the priest in sorrow. In sorrow it had gazed up at him as the eyes spoke appealingly: 'Trample! Trample! It is to be trampled on by you that I am here.'[1]

NEGATIVE THEOLOGY

CHRISTIANITY IS NOT A culture-religion—indeed it isn't a religion at all, properly speaking. It certainly holds the Bible in high esteem, but is not accurately described as a religion of the Book. It would be grossly incomplete, even ridiculous, without an ethic, but it is not a system of morality. The church and a passion for truth belong centrally to this faith, but one cannot say that Christianity *is* the church, or that it possesses the Truth. We might have continued in this vein for a very long time, noting, among other things, that Christianity is neither a tradition of doctrines or dogmas, nor a certain type of piety, nor the collected works of religious sages and prophets, nor the testimonies of martyrs and social activists—the list could go on and on! If our purpose is to identify the core of this faith, and not just describe its actual behavior in the world (which has regularly contradicted its true and avowed vocation and message), we are confronted straightaway by a dilemma: despite our contention that it is not a religion, Christianity

---

1. Shusaku Endo, *Silence*, trans. William Johnston (Tokyo: Sophia University, with the cooperation of Rutland, Vermont: Tuttle, 1969), 276.

has been so thoroughly "soaked in religion"[2] that it is necessary to clear away many misleading representations and rumors of what Christianity is if one is ever to arrive at a positive definition.

To be sure, there are Christians (in North America one is tempted to say that their name is legion!) who are more than ready to tell everyone *exactly* what Christianity is. They are indeed able to answer the question in very short order! Christians with a little more historical knowledge—and a good deal more *self*-knowledge!—would of course be more circumspect. And if one asked any of the truly great and gifted exponents of Christian faith (St. Paul, St. Augustine, St. Thomas Aquinas, Luther, Calvin, Schleiermacher, Barth, Tillich—to name a few) whether they felt they had adequately defined Christianity in their collected works, not one of them, I will wager, would say that they had. Most, indeed, would pale at the very suggestion!

For Christianity is too numinous a reality (not in itself, but on account of what it points to) for knowledgeable Christians to find satisfaction in most attempts to capture it in positive (*kataphatic*) definitions. Apophatic or negative theology, which of course presupposes a rough image or picture (*Gestalt*) of the subject about which it hopes to speak, is a theology made modest by the grandeur of its subject and the concomitant recognition of its own insuperable limits.[3] Negative theology tries therefore to call attention to its subject by negating wrong, misleading, or partial conceptions of its subject. In doing so, it is particularly conscious of such erroneous conceptions as may, in its immediate historical and culture context, have excessive and questionable influence. That is why, in the foregoing, I have chosen the specific topics that I have—culture religion, the Bible, moral codes, the church, and the assertion that Christianity is the true religion. All of these, as we have been at pains to point out, have some real *connection* with Christianity, some of them more prominently so than others. But the error they have in common chiefly is that they are all *components* or *aspects* of Christianity that have been elevated beyond their rightful place in the Christian faith and caused to seem of its essence. In the short dedication to my grandchildren, I attributed this undue elevation of secondary matters to the fact that for a great many people (in some measure for all of us) it is difficult and frustrating to live with the indefinable, the elusive. Whatever

2. Larry Rasmussen describing Dietrich Bonhoeffer's thought on the subject (see the second epigraph of this book).

3. See the afterword.

is greater than we are, beyond us, may fascinate us but at the same time it threatens us; for it makes us nervously aware of our own limitations, and it rebuffs all pretention of control. So we manage these great subjects (in this case, Christianity) by reducing them to something less than what they are. In this way, Christianity becomes believing in the Bible, or adopting certain moral strictures and stances, or equating this faith with our way of life, and so forth. Part of the object of negative theology, then, is to identify such reductionist portrayals of the subject it wishes to understand.

THE SPACE AT THE CENTER

But negative theology has another and finally a more important aim; and that is to create, through the elimination of false alternatives, an intellectual-spiritual zone or atmosphere, as it were, where the reality under discussion can be contemplated with greater openness, a greater readiness to let that reality speak for itself or at very least with a clarity of mind that has been disabused of unworthy presuppositions and prejudices. For want of a better way of naming this procedure, I think of it as forming a space at the center.

Years ago, in a seminar on theological method, one of my graduate students put it this way:

> Negative theology *defines* by creating a space of unidentified territory around that which is being described. This space allows for movement.[4]

In what follows I shall elaborate on this evocative and pithy statement.

When one attempts to understand and state the core meaning of a major but elusive subject—whether that subject is God or one's closest friend, or some complex event or idea; in short some subject that stubbornly refuses to become a mere object; refuses, as it were, to 'stand still and be counted'—one asks oneself whether one cannot perhaps get a little closer to genuine understanding by asking what would have to be eliminated if one hoped even to approach comprehension. That is, one seeks proximity to the positive by way of negation (*via negativa*). As one eliminates one possibility after another, one leaves in outline an unlabeled space at the center of one's discourse where the reality under discussion may be allowed, as it were, to speak for itself.

---

4. Unfortunately I no longer have the name of the student who offered this definition.

Let me exemplify my meaning by considering a specific problem, one by which we are all often puzzled, whether consciously or subconsciously: how, in our relationships with those closest to us, shall we form an understanding of them without robbing them of their freedom and otherness? My relationship with my friend depends upon my having some relatively trustworthy conception of his character; we do not make friends of "unknown quantities"! Yet our relationships also forbid too specific preconceptions of one another, for that would destroy any possibility of friendship. Recognizing that danger, I find over time that I must learn to be open to surprise in my relationship with my friend. His behavior and speech, his unique otherness, makes it necessary for me to reject image after image, conclusion after conclusion. None of my answers to the question of my friend's identity and character does justice to the rich and varied and never quite predictable personality of my friend.

But in rejecting all such answers and guesses, I am silently but surely creating in my mind a space whose boundaries are gradually sketched in through the elimination of false alternatives. In this space, my friend, still undefined and evidently indefinable, may freely, safely occupy a specific place in my imagination, memory, and expectation. I have been prevented from creating a definitive (controlling!) image of him because I've discovered, in the process of trying, that every image I have projected onto him in time proves itself a *graven image*! My friend's reality, which is of course a living reality, always transcends my tentative conclusions about him. He himself shows up again and again destroying, with his disturbing "here-I-am-ness," the bits and pieces, the quick or studied observations and partial truths and hypotheses that I have been tempted to consider adequate images of the person himself. In Martin Buber's well-known language, the *thou* that my friend *is* necessarily and continuously rejects the *it* that I am perpetually tempted to make of him. So in the wake of my repeated failures to define him, I am left with an ongoing contemplation of the ineffable otherness and mystery of his person. And this, frustrating as it is in many respects, is also the condition without which our friendship could not endure. For at the moment in which I believe that I have finally understood my friend ("I know now what makes you tick!"), I shall have in fact robbed him (and myself) of the fascination, risk, and trust that made our friendship possible—made it, in fact, friendship and not some less meaningful relationship. This space at the center, this tentative matrix of our relationship, is thus a matter of extreme significance, protecting not only the integrity of my friend but also the quality of our relationship.

But of course this crucial center space is not wholly *blank*—not simply a carte blanche. If it were mere white space, without any color or contour, without (to continue with this specific example) any hint or clue about the true identity and intention of my friend, I should have to ask myself in all seriousness whether the individual in question could still be thought a friend. Perhaps the relationship itself was merely tentative or had become empty, a mere convention! Without *something*—some intriguing memory, some shared experience, some sign of a *knowing* that transcends mere *knowing about*, the whole idea of friendship would be reduced to a fiction. Rapt attention to the space at the center can only occur if one sees something there that is very real and enthralling, even though it is neither clearly perceptible nor predicable nor fully expressible in images, ideas, or words. Such attention can only endure, however, if it concerns not only my friend but also the significance, to me, of our friendship. Far from being a matter merely of curiosity or vague interest, the relationship entails, for me, a dimension of personal depth, meaning, and basic need.

Now if we can think of the core of Christianity, metaphorically, as the space left at the center after the merely secondary and tangential elements of the Christian religion are ruled out, how shall we speak of the vital something that faith sees there—the compelling command that prevents faith from turning away, as so many have done once deprived of the merely *religious* conventions and habits: the stale, unconvincing reasons for remaining at least nominally Christians?

THE NAME AT THE CENTER

There is no need to equivocate in our response to that question; for in whatever way we choose to formulate it, the answer must be . . . Jesus. There would be no reason for further discussion of the meaning of the term *Christianity* were we not at this point to say that the space at the center is named—must be named—with this particular name. As Paul Tillich wrote in his most systematic discussion of the subject,

> Christianity is what it is through the affirmation that Jesus of Nazareth, who has been called 'the Christ', is actually the Christ; namely, he who brings the new state of things, the New Being. Wherever the assertion that Jesus is the Christ is maintained, there

is the Christian message; wherever this assertion is denied, the Christian message is not affirmed.[5]

Iesus Christos Kurios—"Jesus Christ is Lord": the basic, precreedal confession of the disciple community. It was spoken quietly, covertly often, by the early Christians, because all around them what was being shouted was "Caesar is Lord!" Wherever, and insofar as, the Bearer of this Name is known, loved and trusted, all other centres of alleged ultimacy—not only political authority (Caesar) but all, including precious Christian tenets and symbols that are full of import—are decreased and demoted. For Christians, therefore, neither culture, text, doctrine, moral system, church, nor any distillation of truth can claim our "ultimate concern" (Tillich). *Iesus Christos Kurios*! That Name holds for Christians the same revealing and concealing plenitude that the tetragrammaton YHWH holds for Jews. It negates or relativizes other claimants to finality. For all these others (perhaps the 'religious' ones most of all) would and do enslave the creatures beloved of this Name. The dominion of this Lord is the dominion of love. To be bound by Him, is to be free.

What seems to me so intriguing in our present context is that, precisely as the Christian religion falls into conspicuous decline, if not disrepute (at least in the West), the figure of Jesus remains—and, indeed, becomes more prominent. There is something about that figure, including the remnants of his teachings and his deeds, that continues to enthrall many who otherwise would certainly not regard themselves as religious persons or, specifically, Christians.

It is necessary to ask, however, whether what remains of *Jesus* in this postreligious, post-Christendom context, can endure. It could be little more than nostalgia, or a convenient stop-gap to cover the repressed atheism and nihilism of those who "mourn the death of God"[6] but are afraid to face the death of meaning that accompanies that 'event.' In order to last beyond the residue of twenty centuries of piety, attention to the Name at the centre must entail some definitive or expectant sense of its significance *pro me, pro nobis*—for me, and for us humans. There must be at least a hint of *indispensability* about it.

To test the depth of this new or renewed post-Christendom consciousness of Jesus, I wish to consider briefly two recent writings. Like many other Christians, I have a good deal of respect and sympathy for both authors,

---

5. Tillich, *Systematic Theology* (Chicago: University of Chicago Press, 1957), 2:97.

6. A phrase of Samuel Beckett

chiefly because, unlike the more explicitly Christian apologists and true-believers, they both recognize that the conventional or habitual reasons for religious belief, including Christian belief, have little or no weight with the vast majority of our contemporaries. Both writers turn to Jesus as persons who have in some real or even dramatic sense come to the realization that our time is, or is fast becoming, a time (in Bonhoeffer's sense) of "no religion at all," despite the tumult of myriad religions and quasi-religions in every corner of life.

Jesus the Prophet of Nazareth

Richard Holloway, former Episcopal bishop of Edinburgh, in his much-read book, *Doubts and Loves: What Is Left of Christianity*, contemplates the rise and fall of Christendom. It has been traditional, he says, for historians of Christianity to see the Constantinian-Theodosian establishment of Christianity as the dominant (and eventually the only official) religion of the Roman Empire as a great triumph for a faith that had been persecuted and rejected for three centuries. "So glorious and powerful was the institution of Christendom that it was almost impossible to see through it to the man who stood behind it, the peasant from Galilee who had refused to cringe before the very power that crucified him and was later officially to defy him." Today, he continues, and for the past two centuries or so, when Christendom has been humiliated and, with a few exceptions, reduced to a shadow of its former grandiosity, we are better able to discern what Christianity was and is really all about: "The fascinating thing about our day is that, as the political and theological structures of Christendom crash down before our eyes, we can see once again, through the rubble and dust of the centuries, a clearer picture of the prophet of Nazareth."[7]

It is not necessary to follow Bishop Holloway in all of his interesting pronouncements; but it is necessary and right to follow his lead in naming "what remains"—or, to use my own figure of speech, in assigning to the space at the center a *sufficient* specificity to prevent its being a mere spiritual vagueness. When "the dust and rubble" settles, when the secondary and inessential and trivial aspects of the Christian religion have been negated, the space left at the center can be given only one name: Jesus "the prophet of Nazareth."

7. Richard Holloway, *Doubts and Loves: What Is Left of Christianity* (Edinburgh: Canongate, 2001), 172.

As we have stated earlier, that name is of course, in any case, the only reason we could call the faith we are trying to define *Christianity*. Why else should that noun be employed? Whatever else Christianity may have been, it is inexplicable apart from that name. But, as Bishop Holloway would also insist, that is not the real reason why the tentative and indefinite space at the center should be labeled Jesus Christ. We are not dealing here with semantics only. What keeps men and women—what keeps *us*—from going away with all the others who are going and have gone, is certainly not anything as purely academic as an indelible linguistic connection between the terms *Christ* and *Christianity*. It is infinitely more subtle than that, this enthrallment. It has to do in a vital and gripping way with the actual being, the speaking and doing, the living and dying *of this person*.

We look around, we conjure up what we can remember or discover of the sojourn of the human species on this small planet, and we think: Is there not in *that* life something unique and unforgettable? Can one ever dismiss all that, and the existential challenge that it carries with it? Yes of course; there are other lives, other ways. But whether through historical accident or some more elusive means, this is the life and the way and the truth that has presented its claims to me, and I am not able to ignore it—despite my resistance of it. In this life and the directives it contains I glimpse a way beyond the impasse of my own life, a way into the future.

The question that must be asked about Bishop Holloway's *kind* of response to the end of Christendom and the growing lostness of the West is whether "the prophet of Nazareth" is a sufficiently compelling conception of this 'one who remains' to hold the attention of what Charles Taylor terms *a secular age*. The two-thousand-year tradition of the church's contemplation of the person and work of Jesus Christ certainly includes the office of prophecy; some (and I am one of them) would complain that the prophetic office of the Christ has been the most *undeveloped* of the threefold office [*munus triplex*[8]] of Christian soteriology. With a few exceptions (e.g., the Social Gospel), the priestly and kingly offices have vastly outshone the prophetic. One could ask, as Bishop Holloway and others do, whether the reason for this neglect had something to do with the *radicality* of Jesus's prophetic/teaching role, which, if considered in all seriousness, raises a great many questions about the rich, powerful, priestly, and kingly *church* and the imperial nations that adopted this religion. Nevertheless, the traditions of both the person (Christology) and the work/office (soteriology) of

8. Prophet, Priest and King—following the chief Old Testament narrative.

Jesus Christ had good reasons for not *confining* their contemplation of the Christ either to his *humanity* or to his *prophetic* work. For throughout the tangled and complicated and sometimes (to us!) unintelligible theological and philosophic peregrinations of the councils and pronouncements of the early church, and in medieval and Reformation theologies too, runs the thread of one desperate question: are there, in the believers' remembrances and spiritual experiences of this Jesus of Nazareth sufficient reasons for us to believe that he has put us in touch with the Ultimate—the Absolute—in a manner unique in human experience? It is the same question as the one that John the Baptist addressed to Jesus himself: "'Are you the one who is to come, or are we to wait for another?'" (Luke 7:19, NRSV). Is the Ultimate—is God!—truly present in this mortal, finite and very particular person? That he was *human*—even *truly* human (*vere homo*); human in an exemplary, authentic, and compelling way: this we can readily allow ourselves to believe. But was there, in this truly *human* humanity, also something so luminous and mysterious that it revealed the Unnamable, the ineffable *Divine* in a manner more commanding even than God's Self-manifestation to the great founders of our tradition, Abraham, Jacob-Israel, Moses, the prophets? That he was a *prophet*, we can allow ourselves to believe. But is prophecy the full extent of his work? And if it is not, why should his prophetic teachings and demonstrations claim, to use Tillich's terms, our ultimate concern?

The arguments given by our predecessors—the early councils, the Scholastics of the medieval period, the Reformers, and our own theological forebears—may seem to our ears convoluted and excessive, but we must bear in mind that they were struggling to establish profound reasons why Jesus, of all possible candidates for the distinction, should be preeminent—should be the cornerstone and foundation of faith; should be thought the Christ, the Bringer of New Being (Tillich), of "new life" (Bonhoeffer). For them—for the entire classical tradition, including the Reformers and beyond—it would simply not be enough to speak of Jesus 'the prophet of Nazareth'.

One can agree—enthusiastically!—that Jesus as prophet, as teacher and exemplar of a new and different kind of humanity, has been neglected. Jesus's prophetic office, which in many ways is the *practical* end (*telos*) of the revelation that he brings, was obscured in historical theology by the enormous and complicated ecclesiastical discourse concerning his person and his priestly work, both of which are in a profound sense only (!)

necessary *means* to the realization of that very practical end. But they are, I think, *necessary* means. For, as we have seen in the foregoing, and especially in chapter 4, the realization of that end—that we should hear this prophet and live as he commands—cannot be accomplished by teaching, example and exhortation. *Metanoia* ("rebirth") is its prerequisite—and that is God's possibility, a matter of Gospel not Law.[9]

The Simple Christianity of the Soul

In the 2012 Easter edition of the American magazine *Newsweek*,[10] the English-American journalist Andrew Sullivan, a (former? lapsed?) Roman Catholic, presents an extensive essay titled "Christianity in Crisis," which, in a manner even more explicit than Bishop Holloway's, insists that what Christianity is really about is Jesus. Though Sullivan gives us some puzzling and perhaps contradictory hints about his own relation to the church and its traditions, he wants chiefly to tell us (in the byline of his article) that "Christianity has been destroyed by politics, priests, and get-rich evangelists"; and he advises us to "ignore them . . . and embrace Him [i.e., Jesus]."

Sullivan's essay is rich in evocative comments on the status of our society and our 'Christianity':

- we must "give up power over others, because power, to be effective, ultimately requires the threat of violence,'

- the Catholic Church "lost much of its authority over the American flock with the unilateral prohibition of the pill in 1968 by Pope Paul VI."

- "mainline Protestant churches, which long promoted religious moderation, have rapidly declined in the past 50 years. Evangelical Protestantism has stepped into the vacuum, but it

9. As I listened to a recent CBC (Canadian Broadcasting Corportation) radio interview with Bishop Holloway, I could not help noting how frequently the bishop employed the clause, "if only we could": "If only we could make up our minds to . . ."; "If only we could accentuate the positive aspects of human thinking and achievement . . ." It is a predictably Anglo-Saxon (especially a British) approach to reality. It presupposes a quite Pelagian assumption about the human condition: "We *can* change, so let us please change!" But Augustine, the opponent of Pelagius, would respond, "The trouble is, we can't." I am with Augustine.

10. Andrew Sullivan, "Christianity in Crisis," *Newsweek*, April 2, 2012. Online: http://www.thedailybeast.com/newsweek/2012/04/01/andrew-sullivan-christianity-in-crisis.html/.

has serious problems of its own." It manifests "impulses born of panic in the face of modernity, and fear before an amorphous 'other.'"

- "Given this crisis, it is no surprise that the fastest-growing segment of belief among the young is atheism . . . Nor is it a shock that so many have turned away from organized Christianity and toward 'spirituality.'"

Sullivan's own solution to the crisis of organized Christianity is to return to the kind of Christianity espoused (he argues) by Thomas Jefferson, Francis of Assisi, and his Irish grandmother: the word *simple* appears very frequently in his exposition. He quotes Jefferson: "'We must reduce our volume to the simple evangelists, select, even from them, the very words only of Jesus . . . ,' which are "as 'diamonds' in a 'dunghill.'" "Jefferson's vision of a simpler, purer, apolitical Christianity", he writes, "couldn't be further from the 21st-century American reality. We inhabit a polity now saturated with religion." By contrast, "what [Jefferson] grasped . . . was the core simplicity of Jesus' message of renunciation. He believed that stripped of the doctrine of the Incarnation, Resurrection, and the various miracles, the message of Jesus was the deepest miracle. And that is was radically simple. It was explained in stories, parables, and metaphors—not theological doctrines of immense complexity. It was proven by his willingness to submit himself to an unjustified execution. *The cross itself was not the point [my italics];* nor was the intense physical suffering he endured. The point was how he conducted himself through it all—calm, loving, accepting."[11] (What happened to the cry of dereliction?)

I am attracted to Sullivan's position for one reason—and perhaps only that one reason: namely, its right and necessary insistence that the core of Christianity, to which Christians must return, and which spontaneously appeals to many who are "not of this fold," is Jesus. *His* is the name in the space at the center, and it is not erased or besmirched by all the corruption, stupidity, and bombast of those who *use* that name for their own purposes. Despite "the anxious, crammed lives of our modern twittering souls, the nagging emptiness of our late-capitalist lives," "the cult of distracting contemporaneity," "the threat of apocalyptic war where Jesus once walked," a Christianity that "comes not from the head or the gut, but from the soul . . . and is quietly liberating" remains. In Jesus, it has been there all along;

---

11. Sullivan, "Christianity in Crisis."

"And one day soon, when politics and doctrine and pride recede, it will rise again."

In addition to the strange utopianism of this final phrase—strange, for a man so obviously cynical about our present society—, the vision of Andrew Sullivan has certain serious flaws. They must be commented upon, because they are not the property of Mr. Sullivan alone; they are very common, though Sullivan's way of talking about them is uncommon in the brilliance of its satire. I wish to pinpoint only two of the flaws in this argument:

First, its dismissal of the inept, corrupt church in favor of the pure, apolitical, Jesus-cum-St. Francis-cum-Jefferson et al. As I have argued in chapter 5, Christianity is "Not the Church"; however, the visible, mixed-up, never really faithful church should not, and cannot be, ignored. It cannot even be avoided! Even a Jeffersonian-type piety centered in the "pure, precious moral teaching" of Jesus, as soon as it migrated from the individual soul to a group of like-minded souls would form the basis of a *church*! More important, one suspects some connection between Andrew Sullivan's celebration of personal faith in Jesus and his distaste (to say the least) for Christian political involvement and action? A church, no matter what its theological basis, is in addition to other things a political entity.

Second, the position is flawed in its naivety about the simplicity of the teachings of Jesus and their salvific potentiality. Even if it were true that Jesus's teachings are simple (and they are not), *we* are not simple! We humans, individually and collectively, are such bundles of good intentions and duplicitous if not plain evil actions that the mere exhortation to emulate Jesus is unable to touch us. "The good that we would, we do not; and the evil that we would not, that we do", says St. Paul on behalf of every one of us who is honest about his or her actuality! Christianity cannot be reduced to a system of morality (see chapter 4, above). When, under the tutelage of moralists from Savonarola to Sullivan, faith in Christ is condensed to the imitation of Christ, it appeals only to those who have not—perhaps cannot—know themselves well enough to admit the depths of their need. What we have in Sullivan is another clever but embarrassingly common reduction of Christianity to moral idealism. But it is gospel, and not law, that lost humankind needs and (at its most honest and open) quite patently waits for; and the example of Jesus's "calm, loving, accepting, radically surrendering" conduct of himself on the cross is not gospel. *Contra* Sullivan, the *Cross is* "the point." That is where gospel lies!

THE FACE IN THE SPACE AT THE CENTER

Clearly the name in the space at the center is not enough. If that name is to be distinguished from all the sentimentalism, moral idealism, and other kinds of *religious* uses to which it has been put, it must be seen to relate to the deepest, most abysmal, pathetic, and tragic dimensions of our humanity. The name must acquire a face, and it cannot be the face of a teacher of higher morality, or even that of a prophet only. If it is going to attract *our* attention, it must be a face that knows our weakness and remembers that we are dust. *We*, the quietly desperate majority (Thoreau), the creatures whose most telling self-analyses are some version of Edvard Munch's *The Scream*[12]—we must find our own faces mirrored in that face. If Andrew Sullivan's rhetoric suggests a face, it is the face of Sallman's *Head of Christ* or, at most, Hoffman's *Christ in the Garden of Gethsemane*—pictures that have adorned nearly every sanctuary and classroom in North American Protestant churches; pictures that may uplift spirits already inclined to piety but say nothing to sinners; pictures that may spur on warriors of temperance and moderation and "all things bright and beautiful," but that do not challenge the Moral Majority to seek justice for the poor or healing for the victims of AIDS. Visual representations of Jesus Christ can be even more conspicuously "soaked in religion" than are most verbal representations of the Redeemer. Religious kitsch abounds. We are told that the One praying alone in the Garden of Sorrows brought forth a sweat "like great drops of blood falling on the ground" (Luke 22:44, NRSV). Hardly a "calm, loving, accepting, radically surrendering" exemplar of higher morality!

It is Rembrandt that we need, not Sallman or Hoffmann, and not the glorious Christ images of the Renaissance either.[13] We are the generations

12. It is interesting that the recent sale (for 120 million dollars) of the fourth version of Munch's painting elicited from journalists and art historians the declaration that this is the second most familiar painting in history, outdone only by Leonardo's *Mona Lisa*. Since no *objective* test could render such a judgement, it can only mean that Munch's painting seems to many today to represent the human condition in a gripping and singular manner.

13. For instance, Rembrandt's *Christ in Gethsemane* (Drawing from about 1657 [Valentiner 452]), a meditation on Luke 22:43–44, would be an excellent place to begin in any research on Rembrandt's understanding of Christianity. The great ecumenist of the twentieth century, W. A. Visser t' Hooft, wrote a marvelous book, too little known, on his countryman Rembrandt, which concludes as follows: "Luther makes an unambiguous distinction between a theology of glory and the true theology of the cross. The theology of glory, he says, 'perfers works to suffering, glory to the cross, power to weakness, wisdom to foolishness, and in one word evil to good.' But the theology of the cross knows

after Auschwitz, after 9/11, after Rwanda, after Iraq. The only *imago Christi* that can keep honest human attention fixed upon the heart of Christianity is one in which we are able to recognize in all truth the terror and the beauty, the dereliction and longing of our actual human condition. If the Christ does not share our predicament (that we are "being-towards-death" (Heidegger), that we are perennial betrayers of love, that we live as the despairing who cannot say the word *despair*)—if the Christ does not participate in the "body of *this* death" (Paul), then neither can the Christ liberate us from our bondage to death.

That is why I have chosen for the epigraph of this concluding statement a quotation from the extraordinary novel *Silence*, by the Japanese Christian, the late Shusaku Endo—a writer who, not incidentally, had learned much from the Japanese Lutheran theologian Kazuo Kitamori, theologian of the pain of God. In this quasi-historical novel, Endo, better than any literary artist known to me, describes graphically and with a truly biblical sensitivity *the face*—that is, the spirit and intention, the *passio Christi*—that faith today finds, and *must* find, in *the space at the center*. Of course I look to many other sources for the *discursive* or ideational understanding of the gospel of the crucified one: the divine pathos at the heart of the prophetic literature of Israel (Heschel); the Gospels, and the Epistles of Paul; the works of Augustine and Luther and Kierkegaard; and of many contemporary authors—for I am of course referring to what I called in my first major theological study the "thin tradition" of the theology of the cross:*theologia crucis*.[14] But since I am using the metaphoric language of graphic images here, I turn again, as I have found myself doing constantly for the past four decades,[15] to Endo's unique and gripping story.

In briefest form, it is the story of a young and devout Jesuit priest, sent from his native Portugal to be part of the early seventeenth-century Jesuit mission to Japan. In his seminary training in Portugal, young Father Rodrigues was a model of the pure, unclouded, and sincere devotion to Jesus that his order sought. His piety is centered in the adoration of the

---

that 'it is not enough for anybody nor does it help him that he recognizes God in his glory and majesty, unless he recognizes him in the abasement and ignominy of the cross. In analogy to this we may describe Rembrandt's style as a 'painting of the cross." (W. A. Visseer t' Hooft, *Rembrandt and the Gospel* [London: SCM, 1957], 115–16.)

14. Douglas John Hall, *Lighten Our Darkness: Towards an Indigenous Theology of the Cross* (Philadelphia: Westminster, 1976).

15. See Hall, "Theological Reflections on Shusaku Endo's *Silence*," *Interpretation* 33/3 (1979) 254–67.

person of Jesus. In his mind and heart, he carries a strong image of the face of the Christ. It is a face of pure beauty, resembling that of the Christ figure in a famous painting known to the priest. "'It is a face filled with vigor and strength. I feel great love for that face. I am always fascinated by the face of the Christ, just like a man fascinated by the face of his beloved.'"[16]

There is only one problem: *That face never speaks to the young priest. It remains for him a purely visual and subjective image.*

Then, during the horrific persecutions that marked the missionizing attempts of the Jesuits in seventeenth-century Japan, Rodrigues is captured and imprisoned by the Japanese forces of resistance to this imported faith, a religion that simply does not take root in the "swamp of Japan." A bronze plaque bearing the image of the Christ is brought before him, as it has been presented to all the Christian missioners and converts, and he is commanded to trample on the face in order to indicate that he renounces his faith: for him it would mean, of course, apostasy. The face on the plaque (*fumie*) is not at all beautiful, vigorous, or strong. It has been stomped upon and ground down by the toes of hundreds of defectors and is savagely disfigured.

Heroically maintaining his faith and the honor of the Church, the young priest refuses to trample on the *fumie*. But then he learns that three simple peasants who had been converted but had already apostatized several times, were hanging head down in a pit of excrement and breathing with extreme difficulty. They would be released only if the priest renounced his faith. His personal triumph would mean their deaths.

Faced with such a grim choice, the priest hesitates, his foot poised to move but full of pain. Then suddenly from the disfigured and brutalized face on the bronze *fumie*—the face of one in whom there was no beauty, that we should desire him (Isaiah 53:2)—the distraught young priest hears a *voice*—the voice of a Christ no longer silent.

> And then the Christ in bronze speaks to the priest: 'Trample! Trample! I more than anyone know of the pain in your foot. Trample! It was to be trampled on by men that I was born into this world. It was to share men's pain that I carried my cross.'[17]

Paul Tillich wrote that "the new form of Christianity" cannot "be named yet," though it is "to be expected and prepared for," and "elements

---

16. Endo, *Silence*, 46.

17. Ibid., 271.

of it can be described."[18] I would only like to add to these wise words of my great teacher this: that since these words were written, more than half a century ago, while we are still unable to say with any kind of confidence what "the new form of Christianity" will be, it is by now much clearer what it will not and cannot be. It cannot be the triumphalistic, imperial religion of Christendom. And because, providentially, so much of the "religious top-dressing" (Rahner) and so many of the grandiose visions of the Christian future have been washed clear away by time and the strange turnings of the nearly impossible creature said to be sapientially superior, it is also a little clearer what remains. We may not be able to name the Christianity of the future, but we know better now what Name that Christianity will have to name. And we know better than before, if we have been studying the face of contemporary humankind and the plight of our small blue planet, what kind of face that Name must convey if it is really to speak to us in all the confusion, threat, and fugitive promise of our species. It is the face of "Jesus Christ . . . *and him crucified.*"[19]

+ + +

18. Tillich, *The Protestant Era*, trans. James Luther Adams (Chicago: University of Chicago Press, 1948), xxii (author's introduction).

19. 1 Corinthians 1:23 (KJV).

Afterword

Such knowledge is too wonderful for me;
it is high, I cannot attain unto it.

PSALM 139:6 (KJV)

PERHAPS IT IS NECESSARY to append to this exercise in negative theology a brief caveat: It is only after one has given oneself heart and soul to the task of understanding that one is permitted to confess, "I do not understand." The condition of *not understanding* presupposes a profound—and likely a prolonged—quest for understanding. To state it in other language, apophatic sensitivity assumes a kataphatic background of knowledge. It is one thing for the college freshman to assert that the Bible is not true; it is something else again for the faithful scholar of the Scriptures, who through the biblical words has glimpsed something of the living Word to which they point, to conclude that the Bible is not the Truth.

This book, which I intend to be my last, presupposes the existential struggles of some two dozen previous books (and much besides!), in which I strove to follow the wise directive of Augustine: *Credo ut intelligam*—I believe in order to understand. Understanding presupposes faith, but if there is faith—really faith!—then it makes the effort to comprehend, and it will not give up easily or too soon but will wrestle with the angel of comprehension as Jacob wrestled with the mysterious presence at Peniel. It will demand some small blessing of understanding. And (such is the grace of God) probably it will receive such crumbs of knowledge as it needs—for the time being.

But it will also, like Jacob, leave the struggle limping; for even the little knowledge it has been granted will remind it continually of its woeful inadequacy. Negative theology is the outcome of affirmative theology deeply and faithfully—even doggedly!—pursued.

I hope it will be understood, therefore, that my negations of certain prominent misconceptions of Christianity have been generated neither by a facile dismissal of such views nor by disdain for those who hold them. They are the consequence, rather, of a nagging recognition of the fact that in relation to the mysteries at the heart of this faith, *my own* knowledge is a small, poor thing. Such understanding as has been granted me, scanty as it is, is nevertheless profound *enough* to make me realize, more and more, that the wisdom for which faith sighs "is too high, I cannot attain unto it." At eighty-four, I know what I certainly did not know as well at forty-four, and what I should know even better were I to live another twenty years: that in relation to what is there to be known, I know very, very little.

Lately it has even occurred to me that Christianity as a whole—the entire two millennia of attempts, some obviously mediocre, some courageous and brilliant, to comprehend the gospel of "Jesus Christ and him crucified" (1 Corinthians 1:23; 2:2)—might be nothing more than the history of inept and bungled endeavor on the part of meager spirits to grasp a revelation so blinding in its depth and simplicity that creatures such as we simply could not "attain unto it." What Karen Armstrong calls "apophatic reticence" is not to be confused with the fashionable agnosticism that sophisticated moderns bring to every conversation about religion; it is rather the consequence of a "stunned appreciation of an 'otherness' beyond the competence of language."[1]

And yet—and here one caveat leads to another!—such awareness of the unknown and unspeakable otherness that is the root cause of apophatic reticence should not become an excuse for the failure of the faithful to *strive* for understanding. Above all, it should not function to discourage anyone, young or old, from undertaking . . . *theology!* There is already in the churches more than enough skepticism about theology (what Karl Barth once called "the childhood disease of being ashamed of theology!"). The *conclusion* that Truth transcends and defies definition should not be turned into a *premise.* Apophatic thought about God and the things of God is credible only when it is preceded by persistent—and inevitably frustrating—devotion to the discipleship of seeking a deeper understanding of what we believe.

---

1. Karen Armstrong, *The Case for God* (New York: Knopf, 2009), 320.

+ + +

A prominent aspect of that discipleship is the ongoing dialogue about the faith essential to the life of the Christian community; and this prompts me to acknowledge, finally, the importance of the contributions that have been made to *this* study by the many persons who heard and responded to the addresses in which I first broached its main thesis and themes. The earliest versions of chapters 1, 2, and 4, as well as aspects of the introduction, were presented as the Kaye Lectures of Vancouver School of Theology in 2006. Later these segments were revised for presentation at the Church of the Crossroads in Honolulu, the Plymouth Congregational Church in Miami, and as the Byberg Lectures of the Lutheran Synod in Oregon. In all these settings, I benefited immensely from the responses—including some frank criticisms—of my hearers. The present volume, however, is a complete reworking of the original material, and chapters 3, 5, and 6, as well as the dedication, most of the introduction, and the conclusion, are entirely new.

—DJH

Bibliography

Augustine. *The Confessions of Saint Augustine.* Translated by Edward B. Pusey. New York: Modern Library, 1949.

Armstrong, Karen. *The Battle for God.* New York: Knopf, 2000.

———. *The Case for God.* New York: Knopf, 2009.

Bachman, E. Theodore. Introduction to "A Brief Instruction on What to Look for and Expect in the Gospels." In *Luther's Works*, edited by Helmut T. Lehmann, 35:115–16. Philadelphia: Muhlenberg, 1960.

Barth, Karl. *Anselm: Fides Quaerens Intellectum.* 1960. Reprinted, Pittsburgh: Pickwick Publications, 1975.

———. *Church Dogmatics*, I/1: *The Doctrine of the Word of God, Part One.* Translated by G. T. Thomson and Harold Knight. Edinburgh: T. & T. Clark, 1936.

———. *Church Dogmatics*, I/2: *The Doctrine of the Word of God, Part Two.* Translated by G. T. Thomson and Harold Knight. Edinburgh: T. & T. Clark, 1956.

———. *Deliverance to the Captives.* Translated by Marguerite Wieser. 1961. Reprinted, Eugene, OR: Wipf & Stock, 2010.

———. *Dogmatics in Outline.* Translated by G. T. Thomson. London: SCM, 1949.

———. *Karl Barth, Church Dogmatics: Selections.* Edited by Helmut Gollwitzer. Translated by G. W. Bromiley. 1961. Reprinted, Louisville: Westminster John Knox, 1994.

Bennett, John C. *The Radical Imperative: From Theology to Social Ethics.* Philadelphia: Westminster, 1975.

Berger, Peter L. *The Noise of Solemn Assemblies: Christian Commitment and the Religious Establishment.* Garden City, NY: Doubleday, 1961.

Berkhof, Hendrikus. *Christian Faith: An Introduction to the Study of Faith.* Translated by Sierd Woudstra. Grand Rapids: Eerdmans, 1979.

Bonhoeffer, Dietrich. *Letters and Papers from Prison.* Edited by Eberhard Bethge. Translated by Reginald H. Fuller. London: SCM, 1953.

Calvin, John. *Institutes of the Christian Religion.* Translated by John Allen. Philadelphia: Presbyterian Board of Christian Education, 1936.

Chesterton, G. K. *St. Francis of Assisi.* Garden City, NY: Image, 1957.

Clark, Kenneth. *Civilization: A Personal View.* Harmondsworth, UK: Penguin, 1982.

Clarke, Patricia. "The Relationship between Congregations and the General Council Is . . . Frayed." *United Church Observer*, October 2012. Online: http://www.ucobserver.org/opinion/2012/04/02/relationship/print/.

Dowland, Seth. "Moral Majority." In *The Encyclopedia of Protestantism*, edited by Hans J. Hillerbrand, 3:1306–7. New York: Routledge, 2004.

Ebeling, Gerhard. *Luther: An Introduction to His Thought.* Translated by R. W. Wilson. Philadelphia: Fortress, 1970.

Ellul, Jacques. *Living Faith: Belief and Doubt in a Perilous World.* Translated by Peter Heinegg. San Francisco: Harper & Row, 1983.

Endo, Shusaku. *Silence.* Translated by William Johnston. Tokyo: Sophia University, with Rutland, VT: Tuttle, 1969.

Hall, Douglas John. "The Diversity of Christian Witnessing in the Tension between Subjection to the Word and Relation to the Context." In *Luther's Ecumenical Significance: An Interconfessional Consultation,* edited by Peter Manns and Harding Meyer, 247–68. Philadelphia: Fortress, 1984.

———. *Imaging God: Dominion as Stewardship.* 1986. Reprinted, Eugene, OR: Wipf & Stock, 2004.

———. *Lighten Our Darkness: Towards an Indigenous Theology of the Cross.* Philadelphia: Westminster, 1976.

———. *The Messenger: Friendship, Faith, and Finding One's Way.* Eugene, OR: Cascade Books, 2011.

———. *Remembered Voices: Reclaiming the Legacy of "Neo-Orthodoxy.* Louisville: Westminster John Knox, 1998.

———. "Theological Reflections on Shusaku Endo's *Silence.*" *Interpretation* 33 (1979) 254–67.

———. *Thinking the Faith: Christian Theology in a North American Context.* Minneapolis: Augsburg, 1989.

———. *Waiting for Gospel: An Appeal to the Dispirited Remnants of Protestant "Establishment."* Eugene, OR: Cascade Books, 2012.

Hillerbrand, Hans J., editor. *The Encyclopedia of Protestantism.* New York: Routledge, 2004.

Holloway, Richard. *Doubts and Loves: What Is Left of Christianity.* Edinburgh: Canongate, 2001.

Jenkins, Philip. *The Next Christendom: The Coming of Global Christianity.* Oxford: Oxford University Press, 2002..

Kepler, Thomas S., editor. *The Table Talk of Martin Luther.* New York: World, 1952.

Kerr, Hugh Thomson, editor. *A Compend of Luther's Theology.* Philadelphia: Westminster, 1943.

Lehmann, Paul L. *Ethics in a Christian Context.* New York: Harper & Row, 1963.

Lindbeck, George A. *The Nature of Doctrine: Religion and Theology in a Postliberal Age.* Philadelphia: Westminster, 1984.

McFague, Sallie. *Life Abundant: Rethinking Theology and Economy for a Planet in Peril.* Minneapolis: Fortress, 2001.

McKibben, Bill. "The Christian Paradox: How a Faithful Nation Gets Jesus Wrong." *Harper's* (August 2005) 31–37.

Mead, Sydney. *The Lively Experiment: The Shaping of christianity in America.* New York: Harper & Row, 1963.

Niebuhr, H. Richard. *Christ and Culture.* New York: Harper, 1951.

———. "Reformation: The Continuing Imperative." *The Christian Century* 77 (1960) 249.

Niebuhr, Reinhold. *An Interpretation of Christian Ethics.* New York: Harper, 1935.

———. *The Nature and Destiny of Man.* 2 vols. New York: Scribner, 1953.

Rahner, Karl. *Mission and Grace: Essays in Pastoral Theology.* Vol. 1. Translated by Cecily Hastings. London: Sheed & Ward, 1963.

———. *The Practice of Faith: A Handbook of Contemporary Spirituality.* New York: Crossroads, 1983.

Rasmussen, Larry L., with Renate Bethge. *Dietrich Bonhoeffer: His Significance for North Americans.* Minneapolis: Fortress, 1992.

Richardson, Alan, editor. *A Theological Word Book of the Bible.* London: SCM, 1950.

Ruether, Rosemary Radford. *Faith and Fratricide: The Theological Roots of Anti-Semitism.* 1974. Reprinted, Eugene, OR: Wipf & Stock, 1996.

———. *Gaia & God: An Ecofeminist Theology of Earth Healing.* San Francisco: HarperSanFrancisco, 1992.

Sayers, Dorothy L. *The Man Born to Be King: A Play-cycle on the Life of Our Lord and Saviour Jesus Christ.* 1943. Reprinted with a new introduction by Ann Loades, Eugene, OR: Wipf & Stock, 2011.

Scherer, Paul. *For We Have This Treasure.* The Yale Lectures on Peaching, 1943. New York: Harper, 1944.

Sullivan, Andrew. "Christianity in Crisis." *Newsweek*, April 2, 2012. Online: http://www.thedailybeast.com/newsweek/2012/04/01/andrew-sullivan-christianity-in-crisis.html.

Tillich, Paul. *On the Boundary: An Autobiographical Sketch.* New York: Scribner, 1966.

———. *The Protestant Era.* Translated by James Luther Adams. Chicago: University of Chicago Press, 1948.

———. *The Shaking of the Foundations.* New York: Scribner, 1948.

———. *Systematic Theology.* 3 vols. Chicago: University of Chicago Press, 1951, 1957, 1963.

Uchimura, Kanzo. *Selected Works of Uchimura Kanzo.* Tokyo: Iwanami, 1953

Vidler, Alec. *The Church in an Age of Revolution.* Middlesex, UK: Penguin, 1961.

Vissert t' Hooft, W. A. *Rembrandt and the Christ.* London: SCM, 1957.

Weizsacher, C. F. von. *The History of Nature.* Translated by Fred D. Wieck. Chicago: Univesity of Chicago, 1949.

Wiesel, Elie. *The Town beyond the Wall.* Translated by Stephen Becker. New York: Atheneum, 1964.

Wilson, A. N. *Tolstoy.* Classic Biography. London: Penguin, 1988.

Index of Scripture

Index of Names